THE BEST SKIN OF YOUR LIFE STARTS HERE

Busting Beauty Myths So You Can Find The Best Skin Care Routine

THE BEST SKIN OF YOUR LIFE STARTS HERE

BUSTING BEAUTY MYTHS SO YOU CAN FIND THE BEST SKIN CARE ROUTINE

3RD EDITION

PAULA BEGOUN

WITH BRYAN BARRON AND DESIREE STORDAHL

PUBLISHER'S DISCLAIMER

The intent of this book is to present the authors' ideas and perceptions about the marketing, sale, and use of cosmetics, as well as to present consumers with information and advice regarding the purchase of makeup and skin care products. The information and recommendations presented in this book strictly reflect the authors' opinions, perceptions, and knowledge about the subject and products mentioned.

It is everyone's inalienable right to judge the products and information presented here based on their own criteria and to disagree with the authors. More important, because everyone's skin can, and probably will, react to external stimuli at some point in their lifetime, any product can potentially cause a negative reaction on skin, at one time or another. If you develop skin sensitivity to a cosmetic, stop using it immediately and consult your physician.

If you need medical advice or have a medical concern about your skin, you should consult a dermatologist or physician in your area. The authors are not medical doctors or professional healthcare providers and they do not provide medical advice or medical diagnoses. This book does not offer medical advice or attempt to diagnose or take care of any skin problem, disease, or skin concern or any other health or medical problem or concern. If you have a medical concern or problem with your skin, please make an appointment to see a dermatologist or physician in your area. Do not use or rely on the statements in this book for medical advice, to diagnose any medical condition, or as an alternative to medical advice from your doctor or other professional healthcare providers. Consult a doctor or other professional healthcare provider if you have any questions about any medical matter and seek immediate medical attention if you believe you or others may be suffering from any medical concern or disorder.

Any information provided by the authors is, at best, of a general nature and cannot substitute for the advice of a medical professional, such as a qualified doctor/physician, dermatologist, nurse, or pharmacist. All products mentioned in this book should be used as directed on the product container or on the website from where such products were purchased. Discontinue using any product that causes irritation (e.g., redness, itching, burning, scaling, soreness, or other symptoms).

DO NOT DELAY SEEKING MEDICAL ADVICE, DISREGARD MEDICAL ADVICE, OR DISCONTINUE MEDICALLY PRESCRIBED PRODUCTS BECAUSE OF INFORMATION OR STATEMENTS PROVIDED IN THIS BOOK.

Author: Paula Begoun
Co-Authors: Bryan Barron & Desiree Stordahl
Editor: John Hopper
Art Direction, Cover Design and Typography: Jason Linscott
Layout: Studio Joyce Dekker
Printing: RR Donnelley

Copyright © 2020, Paula's Choice, LLC
Publisher: Beginning Press
Seattle, WA

ISBN: 978-1-877988-42-4

TABLE OF CONTENTS

CHAPTER 1

THE BEST SKIN OF YOUR LIFE STARTS HERE AND NOW...

SMART, SAFE BEAUTY

In the world of beauty, the words "clean," "all natural," and "organic" are so overused it borders on the absurd. Everyone wants to believe the products they use on their skin are safe, and many may fear synthetic ingredients—this book will help you understand the truth. This desire for "clean beauty" has prompted lots of brands to add their notion of what clean means to them. However, there is no uniform definition of what "clean beauty" means. Because labels like "clean" and "natural" aren't regulated, cosmetic brands or stores can define these terms any way they want to, which only adds to the confusion.

Claiming products are "clean" versus "dirty" is not a bad idea, as long as it's not disingenuous. What really matters, for any beauty product, is that it's formulated with integrity, is completely safe when used as directed, and is as effective as possible to help you achieve the skin you want.

The most important thing to know about "clean beauty" is that it should never be about synthetic ingredients versus natural ingredients. Synthetic ingredients can be completely safe, effective, and sustainable, while natural ingredients can be harmful, ineffective, and unsustainable. We have always evaluated every ingredient based on its benefits, on how it is obtained, whether from the earth or in a laboratory, and, more recently, on its environmental impact on the planet.

This type of evaluation is, and always has been, at the heart of every Paula's Choice Skincare product we formulate and the research we've performed for decades—we want everyone to use the best skin care products available and that are proven by published research to work as claimed. That's why we follow what we call *smart, safe beauty*, which means every skin care product you use should contain the most beneficial blend of non-irritating, natural ingredients, along with a smart selection of safe and effective synthetic ingredients.

The reason this is important is because that's what research shows can create healthy, beautiful skin, now and years on. Everyone needs to avoid any and all ingredients, whether synthetic or natural, that research has shown can cause irritation or inflammation, or can damage skin in any way.

Believing that all natural or all organic is the best way to take care of your skin is a myth; we'll explain more about this later in the book. For now, the essential fact is that natural ingredients, even the best ones, cannot address all of skin's complex needs.

This view of *smart, safe beauty* has been part of my passion and mission since 1984, when I wrote the first of my 21 beauty books exposing the truth about what works and what doesn't work in cosmetics—I know, I've been at this a long time. When I created Paula's Choice Skincare in 1995, I continued to follow the research-proven path of *smart, safe beauty*.

Here's a list of ingredients that should not be used in skin care products:
+ 1,4 Dioxane (as defined by European Union [EU] regulations)
+ Abrasive particles (such as pumice, nut shells, fruit pits, salt, or sugar)
+ Alcohol (SD, denatured, isopropyl, or ethyl)
+ Aluminum powder
+ Essential oils (they cause inflammation)
+ Formaldehyde or formaldehyde-releasing ingredients
+ Fragrant plant extracts (they cause inflammation)
+ Methylisothiazolinone and methylchloroisothiazolinone (in leave-on formulas)
+ Nanoparticles (as defined by EU regulations)
+ Phthalates
+ Sodium lauryl sulfate
+ Synthetic dyes
+ Synthetic fragrances (they cause inflammation)
+ Talc
+ Toluene
+ Triclosan

Based on the established and expanding scientific research, here are the skin care product standards that form the basis of how everyone should evaluate the best way to care for their skin:

+ **Science & Truth –** Even when the research and truth are unpopular, we will still tell you what we've learned, and what it means for you. Often the stated benefits of many ingredients are either misleading or false or are based on a misinterpretation of the data, which is not good for your skin.

+ **Highly Effective** – Proven blends of ingredients at effective levels and packaged for stability deliver ideal results every time. Marketing stories and the fear of synthetic ingredients are never as important for skin as what the research really says.

+ **Environmentally Conscious** – We are committed to doing our part to help reduce the world's carbon footprint. We actively support any brand that seeks sustainable ingredients and recyclable packaging if its products are great for skin.

+ **Non-Irritating** – Every product you use must not inflame or irritate your skin. We can't stress this enough, and we'll explain more about this at length (you will be bored with how often we repeat this).

+ **Multi-Faceted Formulas** – Everyone wants a magic bullet; it's a major driver of how many skin care products are marketed as being the fountain of youth. The absolute truth is that no single ingredient, no matter how brilliant, by itself can address skin's complex needs. Almost without exception, products must use an array of ingredients proven to hydrate, defend against environmental pollutants, aid in barrier repair, restore a youthful appearance, fight signs of aging, reduce acne and clogged pores, minimize blackheads, fight inflammation, and prevent sun damage. And even then, there are limitations. This is where reality can be disappointing, but knowing what is and isn't possible can be freeing and beautiful.

+ **No Animal Testing** – We do not support the testing of beauty products on animals at any stage of product development and never will, nor have we or would we hire a third party to do so on our behalf. We are offended when the only research used to assert that an ingredient is bad for skin is based on studies where the ingredient is fed to animals or used on animals bred to get cancer. Not only is it cruel, but such research doesn't translate into how the ingredients are used in skin care products or, more importantly, on how they will affect human skin.

+ **No Jar Packaging** – Research clearly shows that jar packaging causes many active ingredients, predominantly antioxidants and plant extracts, to become less effective over time because they are routinely exposed to air and light. Jars allow these beneficial ingredients to deteriorate once the lid is removed because they let air and light in.

NO FEAR, JUST FACTS

We hate fearmongering. Too often we see ingredients portrayed as being either good or bad for skin, based on research that is taken out of context or on irrelevant research to reach a conclusion for skin health. We are committed to sharing a balanced analysis of independent, peer-reviewed, and industry-relevant research to help you create the best skin care routine possible.

Most important, we will always be transparent about what we share. We continually seek and evaluate new data and research on skin and skin care ingredients. On our website,

PaulasChoice.com, we share the sources of the research we use so you can see exactly why we say what we say.

FROM ME, PAULA BEGOUN, AUTHOR AND FOUNDER OF PAULA'S CHOICE SKINCARE

What is written in this book may surprise you and shock you; you may agree with it or you may disagree. What I can say with the utmost confidence is that the information on every page is based on what abundant current research shows can help you have healthy, beautiful skin (it's even better if you start using great products sooner rather than later, but getting started is what matters).

Everything we write and the extensive research we perform is meant to help reduce your skin concerns by using a step-by-step skin care routine that's truly effective. And it does require a routine because no single product, no matter how well-formulated, can do it all. Skin is just too complicated, and we know more now than ever before about how to take care of it.

This book was compiled by a talented, dedicated team of experts; I just happen to be the one who has been in the world of cosmetics the longest, and I've been writing books about beauty since 1984. If you're not familiar with my work, to put it simply: I've been studying, reviewing, and researching scientific and medical journals about skin care for over three decades. I have a background in science from my university studies, I was a lifestyle reporter in Seattle for four years, and before that I worked for several years as a professional makeup artist and esthetician.

Starting in 1984—and now with this Special Digital Edition book—I've written 21 books on beauty, skin care, makeup, and haircare (the first entitled *Blue Eyeshadow Should Be Illegal*). Several of the books were well over 1,000 pages, with millions of copies sold around the world.

In 1995, I founded Paula's Choice Skincare, a collection of products I formulated with options for practically every skin type and skin concern. Of course, I love my products and, of course, it's my preference for you to consider them when choosing products for taking the best care of your skin. But I also know that there are many beneficial products from other lines that you can choose. My goal has always been to make sure you understand how to take the best care of your skin, no matter whose products you use.

It has always been my mission to help you get the best skin of your life by knowing what you should and shouldn't use to make it easier for you to find the products that are ideal for your skin type and your skin concerns. Again, this is true whether they are my products or someone else's.

MY SKIN CARE JOURNEY

I've had a love-hate relationship with the cosmetics industry from the very beginning. It started with an intense curiosity and passion for skin care and makeup when I was a teenager. My passion wasn't because I was fixated on buying cosmetics for fun; rather, it was about trying to take care of my problem skin, which progressively got worse no matter what I used or which expert I consulted. It was an emotional nightmare for me and, to this day, I still remember the stress and embarrassment of dealing with the skin problems I suffered through as a teen.

It started with terrible acne at age 11, quickly joined by super-oily skin along with debilitating eczema on over 60% of my body. (In school I had to wear gloves to hold a pencil because my hands were so raw and sore from my incessant scratching of the eczema-triggered itching.)

All I wanted at the time were effective products that would do as they claimed. This didn't seem like too much to ask, right? Given how many times I was told, month after month and year after year, how different products would end my struggle, surely *something* would work. However, over the next 20 years, no matter where I turned, whether to cosmetics counters, drugstores, spas, or doctors' offices, almost every product I tried led to disappointment. Despite the promises and claims, my skin rarely showed any signs of improvement, sometimes it got worse! I felt helpless, yet, like most people, that didn't stop me from trying again and again.

Finally, in my twenties, I came to the realization that most skin care claims were either seriously misleading, just plain wrong, or, at best, delusional. I was determined to find the truth about skin and skin care—it became a compulsion, eventually leading me to take my first steps into a career in the world of cosmetics.

It was by no means a straight path, and I had no idea that it would lead me to where I am today. I only knew I was on a personal pursuit, which eventually became a global mission, and I have never wavered from that mission throughout all the years I've been doing this. I didn't want anyone to go through what I went through ever again. Looking back on my evolving career, I believe I've accomplished much of what I set out to do. But I'm not quitting! There's still a lot of work and research yet to be done.

MY LIFE-CHANGING MOMENT!

I started my cosmetics career back in 1977. During my early years working as a makeup artist, as well as selling skin care and makeup products, I didn't know many of the technical details of why so many skin care and makeup products failed abysmally to live up to their claims; I just knew they didn't work as advertised. Often the products' performance didn't even come close to the claims made for the products, but at the time, I had no way to confirm my suspicions; there was no internet as we know it today and consumers didn't own personal computers.

Right around time was when one of the most historic advancements in the world of cosmetics was taking place. In 1977, the U.S. Food and Drug Administration (FDA) finalized the Fair Packaging and Labeling Act, a piece of cosmetic regulation that was about to change the face of beauty forever, and my future as well.

What took place—after many years of legal wrangling and finessing—was the mandatory requirement for all cosmetics sold in the United States to include a complete list of ingredients printed on the product's packaging, in descending order of content (only ingredients above 1% in the United States); that is, the ingredients listed first on the list were included in the largest amounts and the ingredients at the end of the list were present in the tiniest amounts.

It's difficult to imagine now how significant and radical an event that was. The United States passed this regulation in 1977; the next country to mandate cosmetic ingredient labeling was Australia, but not until 1995! Other countries didn't follow suit until 2000 through 2009.

I was thrilled to finally know what was in a cosmetic, but, at the same time, it was frustrating because so many of the ingredient names were indecipherable (many still are—skin care formulation is complicated—even natural ingredients have difficult Latin names that are impossible for most to decipher). Here was this amazing information on the label, but I had no idea what I was reading; on top of that, there were (and are) thousands of different ingredients that a cosmetics chemist could use to make a product. It made my head spin, but it also prompted me to begin my research to learn what it all meant, and then to write my books, and, eventually, create Paula's Choice Skincare.

JUST KNOWING INGREDIENTS ISN'T ENOUGH

As fascinating as it was to finally know which ingredients products contained, I couldn't tell from the label whether those ingredients were genuinely effective, beneficial, or problematic. In other words, although I knew the function of an ingredient in a formula, there were still fundamental and complicated questions remaining when it came to chemistry, physiology, and value for skin.

It was even more difficult to understand what someone should do if they have multiple concerns, like oily skin and signs of aging with occasional bumps or enlarged pores, or dry skin with redness and environmental damage. Many people, including myself, deal with frustrating combinations like this, and it can be incredibly confusing to figure out how to take care of seemingly contradictory skin concerns.

This book will tell you what kinds of brilliant products can be combined in a cohesive routine to address your skin care needs. And it does take a routine; one product can't do it all—it's the quality of all the products you use, from cleansers to treatment products, boosters, serums, moisturizers, and sunscreens, combined that will help you have the beautiful, healthy skin you want.

YOU DO NEED A COMPREHENSIVE SKIN CARE ROUTINE

Most people want one or maybe two products to take care of their skin, but, in truth, skin's needs are more complex than that. If you have sun damage (and we all have some amount, no matter how good we are about trying to protect our skin from the sun), are showing signs of aging, or have inherited skin problems like acne, rosacea, oily skin, dry skin, and everything in between, every product you use matters.

Even if the goal is prevention (which is why it's vital to start great skin care as soon as possible—you're NEVER too young to take great care of your skin—sun damage and pollution affect us all our lives, from birth on), it still takes a full skin care routine. Why and how to do that to address your various skin care needs is what you'll discover in reading this book.

Study after study makes it abundantly clear that you need to consistently use a complete skin care routine to get the best results. One wrong product or not using the best products for your concern can leave you disappointed and your hard-earned money wasted.

WHY IT'S IMPORTANT TO STAY ON TOP OF THE RESEARCH

Skin care myths, misleading information, and folklore can't stand up to what the research over the past 20 years has proven to be true. Even research from just five years ago has evolved and changed what we know about skin and about which ingredients can help repair it and prevent future damage.

When I completed my first book in 1984, and after every book I've written since, I would always think I had finally said it all, and that now people could find their way to having the best skin possible. Twenty-one books later, that obviously wasn't the case, because as countless new studies were conducted and scientific discoveries were published, knowledge about skin care progressed and changed, and so did our conclusions and recommendations about what does and doesn't work for skin.

As the research evolved, we needed to incorporate what the most current studies demonstrated to be true for skin. Endless hours of research meant each new book needed to reflect the most recent, significant, and meaningful information so you could stay informed and be able to take the best care of your skin. The same is true for this book: It contains the most current information about skin care and there are many revelations we will be sharing with you.

Many people ask us: "Why does skin care have to be so complicated?" or "Why do I have to use so many products?" Or sometimes people tell us, "Well, my grandmother only used bar soap and she looked great!" And then there are those who say, "Well, this group of people for hundreds of years had perfect skin and they used nothing on their skin or they used just this one ingredient" (argan and marula oil come to mind as recent examples, but there have been dozens and dozens over the years).

I have no doubt grandma was a beautiful woman and that different groups of people have skin we envy, and it's easy to believe that's because they only use homemade, natural skin care concoctions. However, I would no sooner expect anyone to use a typewriter rather than a computer or to use a rotary dial phone rather than a smartphone just because those devices worked well years ago or someone swears they prefer their typewriter or rotary dial phone.

Like laptops and smartphones, advances in skin care reflect the same level of advancements in terms of innovative and cutting-edge technology.

Here's the bottom line: Don't cheat your skin by accepting myths or anecdotal information about skin care as fact. A handful of years ago, there was little to no information about the need for broad-spectrum sun protection (both UVA and UVB rays, which are killing your skin every day), antioxidants (which are fundamental to interrupting insidious environmental damage), skin-replenishing ingredients (to replace what skin can't produce any more because of sun damage and age), skin-restoring ingredients (to help skin make better skin cells, build collagen, and repair the skin's barrier), treat acne in the way research shows works best, and on and on.

REGRETTABLY, THERE ARE NO MIRACLES FOR SKIN

Don't get us wrong, skin care is beyond exciting, and having great skin is more possible now than ever before. The issue is that despite all the research and new technology, it's important to remember that there are no miracle ingredients when it comes to skin care. This is one of the more difficult truths for people to accept because cosmetic companies endlessly parade new ingredients with elaborate and enticing—and often fabricated—stories about their wondrous effects on skin.

It's not easy to ignore the barrage of inducements and claims about melon extract, plant stem cells, yeast from monasteries in Japan, snake venom, snail slime, rare earth minerals, or some exotic plant extracts that have no research supporting their claims. Even the most brilliant ingredients with stellar research behind them aren't miracles.

Believing there will be a skin care miracle in the next product you buy will be a problem for your skin and your budget. We've seen fad ingredients come and go, some linger longer than others and some just won't go away despite their serious negative effects on skin (essential oils come to mind). Such products and ingredients are mostly just a waste of time, depriving your skin of what can really make a difference.

It's not that new ingredients aren't fascinating or that some haven't proven over time to be very beneficial for skin, but so many times they are just passing fads that are replaced by something new in a few months. You don't want to be a test subject for ingredients or products that aren't proven. Even if the ingredients prove to be amazing (and there are many you'll find out about in this book), as we said and will repeat again and again: skin is too complicated for any single ingredient to be enough. In fact, just the opposite is true: Skin needs a vast array of substances to be healthy, renewed, replenished, and hydrated, and to feel and look firmer and smoother.

THE START OF PAULA'S CHOICE SKINCARE

I am very proud of the more than 150 skin care and makeup products my team and I have formulated for Paula's Choice Skincare over the years. What a remarkable journey it continues to be!

My reason for starting Paula's Choice Skincare was in large part pressure from my friends, family, and readers of my books. They kept asking me to make my own products, products that didn't have all the "buts" and warnings of the other products I reviewed in my book, *Don't Go to the Cosmetics Counter Without Me*. They would say, "You always write 'this product is good, but it's too expensive for what you get, ...but it has too much fragrance, ...but it comes in unstable packaging, ...but there are better products out there.'" They'd practically yell at me, saying: "Just make your own products so we know what to use, otherwise, it's overwhelming, too much to read, and there's no way to really know what's best!" I understood precisely what they were talking about—that's when my mission in life expanded.

So, in 1993, I decided I could indeed make great products that left out all the "buts" and that were loaded with ingredients that research showed were beneficial for skin. The idea for Paula's Choice Skincare was born; the first eight products began arriving two years later, and went up for sale on the internet in 1995!

As you can tell, my enthusiasm for writing my books and information on my websites didn't go away! I couldn't give up what I had been doing for the previous 10 years of my life while writing my books. Skin care information is not only my mission and heritage, but also my legacy. And, as it turns out, writing my books and formulating products for Paula's Choice Skincare enhanced each other in tangible, meaningful ways.

SKIN FRUSTRATIONS ARE UNIVERSAL

My work has taken me to over 25 countries, providing me with the opportunity to give hundreds of media interviews and to hold speaking engagements in places such as Jakarta, Indonesia; Seoul, South Korea; Stockholm, Sweden; Mexico City, Mexico; Singapore; Sydney and Melbourne, Australia; Kuala Lumpur, Malaysia; Amsterdam, The Netherlands; Moscow, Russia; Taipei, Taiwan; Toronto, Canada; Paris, France; Bangkok, Thailand; Hanoi and Ho Chi Minh City, Vietnam; London, England; Mumbai and Delhi, India, and almost every major city in the United States.

What I've learned is that the business of beauty is universally crazy. There's no place in the world where people aren't frustrated about how to take the best care of their skin. No matter where I've been, people are equally concerned about looking younger and having picture-perfect skin.

As a result, I am asked the same questions wherever I go, and I rarely need to change my responses because how you take care of skin to prevent and diminish concerns such as acne, wrinkles, skin discolorations, clogged pores, dry skin, oily skin, and on and on, doesn't change based on where you live, your gender, or your skin tone. Research proves that the key ingredients and the skin care routine you use to manage these concerns work for everyone and all ages. Of course, there are some differences based on gender and age (e.g., men have facial hair to deal with and women over 40 have hormonal changes that affect how their skin functions), but when it comes to the types of ingredients needed to address almost all skin concerns the solutions are nearly universal.

People all over the world want to know why a product they bought didn't work. Why didn't their wrinkles go away? Why didn't their skin flaws change? Why wasn't their skin tone improved? Why are they still getting breakouts, clogged pores, blackheads, or just starting to have those problems? Why do they still have dry, flaky skin after buying so many products promising to make things better? Why is their skin so red and reactive? What are the best anti-aging ingredients? What are the best eye creams that really can get rid of dark circles? Do I know about a recently launched product with a supposed miracle ingredient and does it work? What about ingredients from Morocco, the Amazon, India, Japan, or China, or some other distant place?

During my presentations, I anticipate the moment when a look of understanding begins to appear on the audience's faces as they start to grasp how many myths they have been inundated with instead of the facts about what is best for skin.

What beauty consumers everywhere want is to take the best care of their skin, look younger, and have an even skin tone, with no enlarged pores, bumps, dry skin, and on and on. In each country I visit, without fail, beauty ideals revolve entirely around youthful, flawless skin, and how to get and maintain it. That last point—how to get there—is inevitably accompanied by shared confusion, worldwide. My team and I want to clear up that confusion for you here and now. We want you to know the facts!

CHAPTER 2

SKIN CARE FACTS YOU NEED TO KNOW

WHY YOU MIGHT NOT HAVE YOUR BEST SKIN YET

There are many reasons why you may not have the skin you want; some you can control, others you can't. But there are always things you can do to improve what's happening to your skin. The major causes are ongoing sun damage from not wearing sunscreen every day of your life from birth on (more on that in a moment), your own biology and genetics, aging, midlife changes (peri-menopause and menopause cause significant changes), health issues, environmental assault, using skin care products that contain irritating ingredients or that don't contain beneficial ingredients, and on and on. To one degree or another, all these factors play a part in the complex and continual process of deterioration that occurs both inside and outside the body.

Over time, not knowing how to prevent at least some of the damage from all the factors mentioned above weakens your skin's vitality and health. Everything, from sustaining skin's youthful function to radiating natural skin color, maintaining firmness, preventing congested pores and breakouts, and keeping skin hydrated and smooth—all involve knowing how to take care of your skin.

Understanding what your skin type and concerns are and how to prevent or combat what can or is happening to it is vital, but it's equally important to know what your skin *doesn't* need. That's critical because the very skin care products you are using might be causing or worsening the problems you're trying to avoid or fix.

Even after decades of looking at skin care formulations, it still shocks us that many skin care products can actually cause problems for skin and make matters worse. For example, products claiming to control oily skin often contain ingredients that make skin more oily. Products claiming to be oil-free often contain ingredients that make skin feel greasy. Products claiming that they won't cause breakouts often contain pore-clogging, emollient ingredients. Products claiming to renew skin and that actually contain ingredients that deplete and dehydrate skin. One consistent problem is that daytime moisturizers often don't contain sunscreen, which is a disaster for skin. And then there's the endless parade of skin care products that contain irritating skin care ingredients, especially essential oils (one of the worst offenders we repeatedly see); irritation is always bad for skin.

YOUR SKIN'S EXPOSOME

Throughout this book, we will repeatedly warn you about how the environment, nutrition, pollution, smoking and second-hand smoke, illness, lifestyle choices, climate, and the skin care products or devices you use cause irritation and are detrimental for skin. The association among all these negative influences now has an official name: exposome factors.

The United States Centers for Disease Control and Prevention (CDC) defines exposome as the measure of everything you will be exposed to from birth to the end of life that can be the source of health problems. It is a new and complex area of study. One branch of exposome research we are excited about is exploring how exposome factors are aging your skin, triggering breakouts, and causing numerous other skin disorders.

In some ways, exposome factors for skin are easier to identify and evaluate than factors for other parts of the body because skin is so quickly and negatively affected by the unhealthy things to which it is exposed. Although you're unlikely to see the real-time damage on the skin's surface from unprotected sun exposure, pollution, unhealthy lifestyle, or the damage irritating skin care products are causing, it can still be quantified. For example, while you can't see the damage that one minute of unprotected sun exposure causes on the surface of skin, you can measure the inflammation it causes by looking at the lower layers of skin with non-invasive testing methods.

WHAT ARE THE BEST INGREDIENTS?

We get asked this all the time and our answer is always the same: There are lots of great ingredients and although there are superhero ingredients to know about, there is no single best one. Aside from the fact that there are literally thousands of different ingredients that can be included in a skin care product, there's no way to sum up which are the best when there are so many worthy, astounding ingredients or, even better, combinations of great ingredients. Then there's the basic fact that different ingredients are better for certain skin types and concerns.

We wish skin care were as easy as finding the best skin care ingredient or even one skin care product that can do it all, but it's not that easy. Skin is the largest organ of the body; it includes a vast range of substances and a beyond-imaginable number of physiological processes and interactions that keep it young, radiant, smooth, healthy, bump- and clog-free, and even-toned (no redness or brown patches). It takes more than one product to handle what is taking place.

But don't be disheartened. Although there isn't any one best ingredient for skin, there are groups of amazing ingredients and categories of ingredients that are critically important for having the best skin possible. With lots of ingredients to choose from, and lots of different combinations, these are just short of being phenomenal for skin!

Here's what happens: When skin's extensive endogenous system of protective ingredients ("endogenous" means the ingredients found naturally in everyone's skin), which are abundant when we're young, start to quickly diminish because of sun damage, pollution, aging, inherited skin disorders, midlife changes, or using irritating or abrasive skin care products, it results in unwanted consequences that worsen with time.

These vital groups of natural protective ingredients in healthy, young skin are primarily antioxidants, skin-replenishing ingredients, and skin-restoring ingredients. The goal is to prevent these substances from being depleted and to replenish them when the damage has already started to occur.

Antioxidants in both the inner and outer layers of skin have repairing properties and help interrupt the terrible free-radical damage caused primarily by pollution and the sun. The naturally-occurring antioxidants in skin include vitamin C, ubiquinone, vitamin E, vitamin A (retinol and its derivative retinyl palmitate), polyphenols, carotenoids, superoxide dismutase, and on and on. There is impressive research showing how oral supplements high in antioxidants protect skin from the inside out against environmental damage and even from sun damage.

Skin-replenishing ingredients are distributed throughout the layers of skin and help protect and repair skin's barrier. They are imperative for hydration and radiance, and significantly impact the smooth look and feel of skin. These naturally-occurring skin-replenishing ingredients include ceramides, triglycerides, glycerin, hyaluronic acid, lecithin, sodium PCA, a vast number of fatty acids (notably omega-6 fatty acids), lipids, cholesterol, amino acids, and glycosaminoglycans.

Skin-restoring ingredients are also plentiful in young skin and continually repair the damage caused by the environment and other factors that keep it from being healthy and young. These important ingredients include vitamin B3 (niacinamide), vitamin A (retinol), peptides, hyaluronic acid, lecithin, adenosine and its derivatives, and some ceramides.

The antioxidants, skin-replenishing ingredients, and skin-restoring ingredients mentioned above are created naturally by the body and are distributed to skin from the inside; however, there are dozens more of these types of ingredients that don't occur naturally in skin, but that can be applied to enhance what the naturally-occurring substances do. These ingredients include plant extracts, plant oils, vitamins, minerals, and lab-created stable versions of antioxidants, skin-replenishing ingredients, and skin-restoring ingredients.

In addition to these ingredients, skin also needs **sun protection and non-abrasive gentle exfoliation,** but we'll get to those in the next chapters.

This combination, in a consistently applied skin care routine, gives skin exactly what it needs for maintenance, rejuvenation, and revitalization.

WHAT ABOUT NATURAL INGREDIENTS?

Natural, naturally-derived, organic, and synthetic ingredients are a polarizing topic. Some people devoutly believe that the best way to take care of their skin is to use skin care products that contain only natural or organic ingredients. This belief persists despite the fact that research clearly shows it isn't true.

The fact is there are lots of natural ingredients that are brilliant for skin, but there also are lots of natural ingredients that are bad for skin, and these show up in skin care products all the time. Also, there are lots of synthetic ingredients that are brilliant for skin and there are no all-natural equivalents for them. Yet, because they are laboratory-created (that is, synthetic), they are not included in products claiming to be all natural (though sometimes companies sneak them in anyway).

Again, natural does not necessarily mean better and synthetic doesn't mean bad! More to the point, there has been no standard set for what constitutes a natural ingredient in a cosmetic, so everyone just makes up their own definition. Moreover, a plant or a mineral still comes out of the ground, and must be processed, cleaned (who wants fertilizer on their skin?), debugged, preserved, and then mixed into a formula and preserved once again. Whether or not that product is still natural after all that processing is up for debate. The problem is that a lot of people make assumptions about this that often are untrue.

That is why we continually pore over the research literature, so we can relay to you the information you need to ensure you are using only products that contain what's proven to help skin and avoiding products that contain ingredients that are over-glorified, that can't perform as you're told, or that no one should be using on their skin. Sadly, many cosmetic companies tout their natural ingredients as the best for skin and claim that synthetic ingredients are killing it; such statements are just misinformation. The companies formulate these very real-sounding claims based on research that's misinterpreted or taken out of context.

Regulatory boards around the world and the United States Department of Agriculture (USDA) have stated repeatedly that people should not interpret any natural or organic seal of approval on cosmetics as proof of health benefits, safety, or efficacy. Such seals are not about the efficacy or safety of the ingredients as used in cosmetics. Whether something is natural and/or organic has no bearing on whether it's good or bad for skin.

One confusing aspect of the natural ingredient discussion is that some of the plant extracts we warn you about do have research showing they have positive properties for skin. The reason we still want you to avoid them is because there is also research showing they can negatively affect skin.

The question is: Why use natural ingredients like witch hazel, lemon, peppermint, alcohols (SD or isopropyl alcohol—other types are fine), lavender, thyme, eucalyptus, tea tree oil, any essential oil, and so on, which have problematic effects, when other plant extracts have only the good stuff and none of the bad?

Natural ingredients can be brilliant for skin, but they also have limitations. Plant extracts and minerals aren't adept at breaking down into a form that can have an effect on the deeper layers of skin. Plants are also inherently not very stable; think of how long a head of lettuce lasts in your refrigerator. Additionally, the quality of plant extracts varies depending on weather conditions, harvesting, and the effects of the processing. There also are things synthetic ingredients can do that strictly natural ingredients cannot. In the world of skin care the research is clear: Taking the best care of your skin involves a smart balance of both natural and lab-engineered ingredients.

Natural ingredients to avoid:

+ Alcohol
  (SD, denatured, isopropyl, or ethyl)
+ Allspice
+ Almond extract
+ Angelica
+ Arnica
+ Balm mint oil
+ Balsam
+ Basil
+ Bergamot
+ Cinnamon
+ Citrus juices or oils
+ Clove
+ Clover blossom
+ Coriander oil
+ Cottonseed oil
+ Cypress
+ Fennel
+ Fir needle
+ Geranium oil
+ Grapefruit
+ Ground-up nuts or shells
+ Horsetail
+ Lavender oil
+ Lemon
+ Lemon balm
+ Lemongrass
+ Lime
+ Marjoram
+ Oak bark
+ Papaya
+ Peppermint
+ Rose
+ Rosemary
+ Sage
+ Thyme
+ Witch hazel
+ Wintergreen
+ Ylang-ylang

Natural ingredients worth considering (there are many more, but this is a good overview):

+ Aloe
+ Amino acids
+ Argan oil
+ Bisabolol
+ Canola oil
+ Carnauba wax
+ Ceramides
+ Chamomile
+ Clays, including kaolin
+ Cocoa
+ Coconut oil
+ Grapes
+ Green tea
+ Honey
+ Hyaluronic acid
+ Licorice
+ Meadowfoam oil
+ Oats
+ Olive oil
+ Omega fatty acids
+ Pomegranate
+ Rice bran oil
+ Rosa canina fruit oil
+ Safflower oil
+ Seaweed (algae)
+ Shea butter
+ Soy (all forms)
+ Sunflower oil
+ Turmeric (curcumin)
+ Willow herb

DON'T TRY IT ON YOURSELF

People often ask why they shouldn't just try a product to see if they like it or why they shouldn't just rely on someone else's experience with a product to decide if it might work for their needs. We can't think of a bigger mistake for your skin than to rely solely on trying a product to see if it works or to determine the benefit and/or quality of the product.

We're not saying you shouldn't use a product you like, but you should make your selection only from the best-formulated products that are right for your skin type. How a product feels on your skin or someone else's skin doesn't give you the crucial information you need about the quality of any formula.

Mainly, what's wrong with applying a product to see if it works is that for many products, you simply can't tell in the short term (and you have to wait a long time for the long term) if it's helping or hurting your skin. And, if it's hurting your skin (you can rarely see the problem happening on the surface and certainly not in the lower layers of skin), why would you want to damage your skin with any product, even for a day, a week, or worse, months?

We know this sounds contradictory, but just because you like the way a product feels on your skin doesn't mean it's a good product, for you or for anyone else. You may like the texture or the look of the product, you may love the way it smells, but that doesn't tell you anything about whether it's beneficial or harmful for skin. For example, if you're not wearing sunscreen every day, you might not feel or see the damage daylight causes, but it's happening, and it starts within the first minute unprotected skin is exposed to daylight.

Think of skin care like your diet: It's easy to like what isn't good for you, whether in the short term or long term. You certainly can't tell from eating chocolate cake that it's a problem for your health or that kale is good for you. If you didn't know better based on the research, who wouldn't eat chocolate cake or some other indulgent food at every meal?

It's important to realize that skin care products can have positive or negative effects and that the negative results can take years to show up. The benefits of a healthy diet don't show up immediately; the same is true for a unhealthy diet, where it can take years before you see the resulting negative effects.

You don't have to risk testing a bad skin care product any more than you need to test smoking a cigarette to find out that it's bad for you because the research has already been done. In the world of skin care, a vast amount of research already has gone into determining which ingredients and formulations are good for skin and which are bad. Knowing that, you just need to determine what ingredients work for your specific skin type and concerns.

To sum it up: How skin care ingredients are combined and how they work in products and on skin has been established in extensive, documented medical and scientific research. The information we present about ingredients is based on that research. That's why our recommendations can really help you find products that work for your skin type and your skin concerns. The best part? You will enjoy using such products because they really work!

HOW CAN YOU UNDERSTAND AN INGREDIENT LABEL?

We wish we could teach everyone how to understand an ingredient label. That's where the fundamental information for determining the effectiveness and functionality of almost any skin care product lives. The ingredient list is the code to determining whether or not a product's claims make any sense and whether it's problematic or beneficial for your skin. But, deciphering an ingredient list is not easy unless you have a background in cosmetic science or cosmetic formulation.

The major limitation in decoding the ingredient list is the sheer number of ingredients in cosmetic formulations. There are literally thousands of ingredients and thousands upon thousands of potential combinations of those ingredients.

Even more confounding are the chemical names of the ingredients, which are, at times, far too technical for most to understand. How can someone without a cosmetic chemistry background ever hope to comprehend what polymethylsilsesquioxane, palmitoyl hexapeptide-12, or cetyl ricinoleate are, let alone understand what they do? Even plant extracts have names that are incomprehensible, such as *Gaultheria procumbens* or *Simmondsia chinensis* (and the stems, seeds, flowers, or leaves of each plant, often with different Latin names, which can make a difference in what they can and can't do).

Vitamin C is a great example. It's one of many wonderful ingredients for skin, but there are over a dozen different forms of it, with overly technical names on an ingredient list. Each one has its own benefit and usefulness in a formulation, and it's not uncommon for more than one form to show up in one product.

We're sometimes asked: How can anyone tell if a product is good by merely reading the ingredient list because don't the concentrations also matter? How can we tell how much of any one ingredient is in a product or the efficacy of the combinations in a specific product? We can because of the research and chemistry we are immersed in. It's sort of like being a master chef. Someone who is an expert in cooking can look at a recipe and quickly grasp the nuances, the ways it can be adapted, and if it will taste good or bad. For skin care, our knowledge of ongoing research about ingredients and the fundamentals of cosmetic chemistry makes it possible for us to understand an ingredient label.

INGREDIENT FEARS

In addition to the difficulty in untangling an ingredient label and all the claims espousing an ingredient's or product's benefits, there are also all the horror stories about ingredients that you find on the internet and from other sources. Almost without exception, the fearmongering about ingredients such as parabens, silicones, mineral oil, certain sulfates, and so on is just plain wrong. But, when something is repeated over and over again, no matter how false, it's very hard to undo.

Sometimes statements made about these types of ingredients (and many, many others) are taken out of context from the research, leading to irrelevant and silly conclusions. Sometimes the statements are made up out of thin air, derived or extrapolated from unrelated sources, or have no scientific basis (you'd be surprised how often this happens).

Any ingredient can be made to sound scary by manipulating the facts. For example, water's chemical name is *dihydrogen monoxide*, which has been confused repeatedly with the dangerous carbon monoxide because the two have similar-sounding technical names.

To demonstrate how such fearmongering works, we'll use mineral oil as an example. There are those who want to scare you into believing that mineral oil is bad for your skin, while research reveals just the opposite. Not only is cosmetic or pharmaceutical-grade mineral oil natural (it comes from the earth), but the research makes it crystal clear that it is one of the most gentle and safe skin care ingredients for dry skin. But, because it is associated with gasoline (petroleum) and in its unpurified form contains benzene, it is falsely labeled by some as the source of all evil for skin.

The fearmongering about silicones is also incredibly disappointing as they are a brilliant group of ingredients that have been used for decades in hospitals around the world for wound healing due to their distinctive skin-protectant and hydrating properties.

And don't get us started on parabens; these are not problematic for skin, and they do not cause disease. Parabens are some of the safest, most non-irritating preservatives ever used in cosmetics (they are found naturally in many plants and berries).

We have more information about these and hundreds more ingredients in our Cosmetic Ingredient Dictionary on PaulasChoice.com, where we directly quote the research and take nothing out of context, providing you with the balanced information you need.

NOT BEING GENTLE IS YOUR SKIN'S WORST ENEMY

We can't stress this enough. The research is abundant and without contradictions (something that rarely happens in science): Not being gentle to your skin is really, really, *really* bad. Most cosmetic companies never talk about this!

In addition to the enormous daily assault our skin suffers from pollution and sun damage (if not using products loaded with antioxidants and a product with an SPF 30 or greater), applying skin care products that contain irritating ingredients or have a harsh texture is also detrimental.

These types of attacks hinder skin's ability to stay hydrated, replenish itself, keep its surface intact, and maintain support structures to keep them from breaking down, among many other complications. Not being gentle also leads to premature aging of the skin and makes any skin problem worse.

For those with oily skin, it's incredibly important to be aware that not treating your skin gently can trigger an increase in the amount of oil coming from the pores and make the pores bigger! That is not good for any skin type!

It turns out that much of what we know about skin aging, the appearance of wrinkles, uneven skin tone, how skin renews itself, and what causes breakouts is based on our increased understanding of what results when skin is inflamed or irritated. Anything that triggers inflammation or irritation will trigger a negative response in skin, which has cumulative negative results. Being gentle is the starting point for having the best skin possible, no matter your skin type or concern.

INFLAMMATION IS SKIN'S SILENT KILLER

It would probably be easier for those who smoke cigarettes to stop smoking if the damage it was causing on the inside showed itself instantly on the outside. Regrettably, that isn't the case; as we now know, it can take years for the cumulative damage to show up. Interestingly, the same can be said for what happens to skin when you do things that have a negative impact.

People often assume their skin care products aren't hurting or aggravating their skin because they don't feel or see any negative reactions on the surface. Unfortunately, regardless of what we see or feel on the surface, there are serious negative things happening in the lower layers of skin when skin is being inflamed. Skin is very good at hiding damage! When the damage taking place beneath skin's surface continues without interruption, it becomes harder and harder to heal.

You can get a clearer idea of how using products that aren't gentle cause this hidden, secret damage by understanding how skin reacts to unprotected sun exposure. Actually, daylight exposure, because indirect sun exposure, even in the shade or on a cloudy day, still damages skin.

The sun is a major cause of early signs of skin aging and skin cancer. Yet, other than the (hopefully) rare occasion when you get sunburned, you won't feel or even see the damage being done to your skin by not wearing a sunscreen, rain or shine, until later in life. Even more shocking is that the most damaging rays of the sun can come through windows, and it's for certain you never feel that—now that really is a silent killer!

Whether it's sun damage, environmental damage, or using skin care products that cause inflammation and irritation, avoiding these is a huge step to getting the skin you want.

SMELLS LIKE TROUBLE FOR YOUR SKIN

Let's start with a fact you may find surprising (or even shocking): Essential oils are bad for skin, period! Now to the details ...

Most of us are attracted to a pleasant fragrance. In fact, the first thing most people do when considering just about any skin care or hair care product is to smell it. As nice as it is to have a product with a wonderful aroma, whether it's coming from essential oils, fragrant plant extracts, or synthetic sources, it's probably terrible for skin. With very few exceptions, what pleases your nose is a problem for your skin.

Fragrant ingredients have a scent because of the volatile compounds they contain. On your skin, these compounds trigger a reaction that causes inflammation, and, for most people, this damaging inflammation is not visible on skin's surface. Research has long established that fragrant ingredients in skin care products are among the most common cause of negative skin reactions. Products that omit volatile, fragrant ingredients are always the best way to go for all skin types.

Unfortunately, your nose cannot always determine from the smell of a product whether it contains problematic fragrant ingredients. Many beneficial skin care ingredients that are completely gentle have a natural, pleasant aroma and do great things for skin. Distinguishing between the ingredients that do wonderful things for skin and the ingredients that are added to make you "shop with your nose" but can cause problems for your skin is not easy.

Like anything in skin care, the most valuable information is on the ingredient label, but because those ingredients read like an advanced college degree in cosmetic chemistry, they are often difficult if not impossible to decipher. Essential oils and fragrant plant extracts can have equally baffling names on an ingredient list. Our job is to help you avoid ever putting those types of products on your skin.

EVERYONE HAS SENSITIVE SKIN

Everyone, to one degree or another, has temperamental skin; that is, our skin reacts negatively to the environment and can react negatively to what we put on it. Regardless of your skin type or concerns, lots of things can upset our skin—some we can avoid and some we can't.

What everyone can do is diminish much of the potential harm by using great skin care products that are loaded with beneficial ingredients, are gentle and soothing to skin, and protect skin from sun damage and pollution. Not doing this weakens skin in so many ways, it's devastating to contemplate.

No matter how you believe your skin reacts to different aspects of the environment and to the products you use, we are all vulnerable to negative reactions if we use skin care products that aren't gentle and if we don't protect our skin from the sun and pollution.

Irritating and inflaming skin is bad for everyone, no matter your ethnic or cultural background. Everyone, everywhere, at every age should be gentle to their skin because using irritating skin care products is detrimental, no matter who you are or where you live.

AGE, SKIN COLOR, OR WHERE YOU LIVE ARE NOT SKIN TYPES!

We know that may be hard to believe considering how often you've read statements to the contrary, but facts are facts, and your age, skin color, ethnic background, and geographic locale are not skin types and they have only a minimal impact on any aspect of how you address your skin care concerns and needs.

It's not that older skin isn't different from younger skin (though to a large extent that depends on how much unprotected sun exposure you've had or when you start going through hormonal changes) or that darker skin color isn't different from lighter skin color, but when it comes to fighting signs of aging, acne, oily skin, dry skin, or protecting skin from sun and pollution damage and so on, research shows that there are minimal differences in what you should and shouldn't do to take care of your skin.

Think of it like your diet: Regardless of our age, ethnic background, skin color, or where we live, we all still need the same types of nutritious foods to be healthy. The exact same concept applies to skin and there's no research to the contrary. Everyone's skin needs the same types of ingredients to address dryness, acne, wrinkles, sun protection, uneven skin tone, oily skin, redness, sensitive skin, and so on.

LIFELONG RULES FOR SKIN CARE SUCCESS

The most important way to achieve the best skin of your life is to obey the following fundamental rules of great skin care ...

Be consistent. For best results, a great skin care routine should be used regularly. Some products you may need to use once or twice daily, others every other day, some once or twice weekly, but, regardless of how often, consistency is imperative.

Apply products in the right order. This is more important than people think. For example, sunscreen should be the last product you apply in your morning skin care routine before you apply your foundation and other makeup. This is very important because you don't want to dilute the sunscreen with the other skin care products you're using.

As a rule, the order of application for any skin care routine is cleanser, toner, and then a leave-on exfoliant. Next, apply the serums, boosters, treatment products, and/or moisturizers based on their texture. The thinnest liquid/fluid products go on first, the thicker ones follow. Generally speaking, there is no need to wait between applying products. Ingredients will absorb into skin on their own because, for the most part, ingredients absorb into skin based on their molecular structure and the delivery system used in the formula. The only reason to wait is if you find that the texture or finish of two products you like to apply at the same time tend to counteract each other, resulting in rolling or balling up on skin. In such a case, waiting for one product to absorb before applying the other often resolves the issue.

Never massage, pull, or tug at skin. The belief that massaging or using any type of roller helps ingredients absorb into skin is a serious mistake for your skin. If you see or feel your skin move, whether up or down, sideways, or in a circular motion, you are aging your skin and setting the stage for it to sag much sooner. This is a physiological fact, because the movement of skin in any direction stretches the delicate elastin fibers that give skin its bounce, allowing it to return to its natural shape. But over time, the elastin fibers in skin work exactly like a rubber band—they stretch out, stop going back to their original shape, and eventually break, resulting in sagging! And, unlike collagen, mature normal elastin fibers are almost impossible to regenerate (you can generate baby elastin, called tropoelastin, which is great, but tropoelastin is not as supple or strong as full grown elastin).

There is no benefit to be gained by aggressively massaging facial skin; it doesn't help firm or contour skin or let ingredients penetrate better, and it doesn't help facial lymph drainage. All the pulling and tugging at skin won't help one iota! Besides, you don't need all ingredients to absorb into skin because that would not be good skin care.

The best products contain some ingredients that stay on the surface of skin (if they absorb, how will they protect the skin's barrier from the environment?), other ingredients that penetrate a little deeper (on their own because of their molecular size), and still others that go deeper where they can reinforce and hydrate the lower layers of skin. Finally, some ingredients penetrate deep enough to help repair and restore (to the extent possible) skin's support structures.

Jade rollers fall into the category of massage being a problem for skin. These are a trend in skin care that, at the very least, are a waste of time and, at their worst, are bad for skin. Jade rollers are handheld devices that hold a smooth stone, which may or may not be made of jade; most are not really jade because pure *jade* is very, very expensive. Even if the material were jade, it doesn't have any special properties for skin ... none whatsoever. As the name suggests, these devices are meant to be rolled over skin, with the stone causing a pleasant cooling sensation.

Jade rollers are touted as a remedy for just about every skin concern under the sun, from wrinkles to puffiness, dark circles, firming, face slimming (yes, face slimming), detoxing skin, as well as helping skin care ingredients absorb better.

Many of these claims are attributed to the massaging action, which is claimed to help improve lymphatic drainage and circulation. What's silly about that is that people don't have lymphatic issues in their face because there are only a few lymph nodes present there. Even if it did help with lymph drainage, any benefit would be temporary at best, and there's no research showing lymph is a problem for facial skin.

The bottom line: Massaging skin can overstimulate circulation, worsening such issues as sensitive skin, rosacea, and broken capillaries, and increasing sagging, and it does not help push ingredients into skin.

Don't expect instant results from almost any skin care product. When it comes to skin care, patience is a virtue. Some products can deliver striking results overnight, but they are the exceptions. It takes time for most products to really make a difference, and maintaining those results requires ongoing use.

For example, products to brighten skin and create an even skin tone can take three to six weeks to begin showing positive outcomes (assuming they are well-formulated, and you are also using a sunscreen every day and not tanning, indoors or outside). Most people won't see the full results until around the three-month mark, and even then, ongoing use is necessary to maintain results.

Products meant to protect, replenish, and defend skin against signs of aging and other problems may show instant hydration, a reduction of fine lines, and increased smoothness, but the significant underlying benefits will be ongoing over the long term, and not necessarily apparent in the short term.

In the short term, using sunscreen every day will make an immediate dramatic difference in how skin heals, restores collagen, repairs underlying damage, and improves skin tone and skin discolorations, but only if you apply it daily. The long-term benefit of using sunscreen daily will become astonishingly evident later in life when you compare your skin to the skin of others who didn't protect their skin from the sun. Then you will be thrilled you followed our advice!

You must "nourish and feed" your skin twice a day. As you age, and mostly because of sun damage from not wearing an SPF 30 or greater every day, your skin cannot naturally replenish the substances it needs to be healthy. Great skin care products give those essential substances back to your skin.

Antioxidants, skin-replenishing substances, and skin-restoring ingredients get used up quickly by skin and must be resupplied on a continual basis, twice daily. Don't cheat your skin by not giving it the indispensable ingredients it needs to maintain a beautiful, healthy appearance, now and for years to come.

Skin doesn't renew itself only at night. We hear repeatedly that "skin renews and repairs itself at night" and, therefore, needs special ingredients at night to help the healing process. Supposedly, these special ingredients aren't necessary during the day, but this isn't even remotely true. In fact, research shows just the opposite is true: Skin actually heals *better* during the day than it does at night because during the day, you are moving around more, increasing blood flow and oxygen intake, which, in turn, stimulates healing far more than just lying still in bed.

In truth, skin needs help, day and night, to renew itself and minimize or prevent other concerns from arising, and there is not a shred of research showing there are any special ingredients your skin needs at night that it doesn't need during the day. The only difference is that during the day you need sunscreen ... everything else can be day or night, preferably both.

One product can't do it all. We've already said this, but it bears repeating. All skin types and concerns require a variety of products to give you the best skin of your life. For some people, the essential products can be limited to cleanser, gentle leave-on exfoliant, sunscreen for daytime, and moisturizer at night. But, if you have special skin concerns or a difficult skin type, you'll need to address those with specialized products designed for the specific problems. Layering targeted solution products specially designed for your skin concerns is the optimal way to get the best results possible.

Regularly use a gentle leave-on exfoliant. The benefit to your skin of a gentle leave-on exfoliant with AHA (glycolic, lactic, malic, or tartaric acids) or BHA (salicylic acid) can be astounding ... many people see results overnight. Helping skin naturally shed the buildup of dead surface cells without any abrasion or harsh scrub particles can make all the difference in the world. The feeling of smoothness you will experience from the first day you start using a gentle leave-on exfoliant will surprise you.

Keep in mind that sun damage, skin disorders, aging, or some inherited skin problems cause skin to shed improperly, and that never goes away; if anything, it gets worse over time. An AHA or BHA exfoliant is a maintenance step that you must use regularly to maintain smooth, radiant skin.

The change in seasons does not necessarily mean you need to change your skin care products. What you need to do is pay attention to when your skin changes regardless of the season. There are all sorts of things that can cause your skin to change seemingly overnight, and that have nothing to do with the weather.

Many people are aware of how hormonal changes affect their skin; others experience skin differences when midlife changes start taking place or when stress shows itself on your skin. The goal is to treat the skin you have now, not the skin that an article you read says you may have because the season changed or you had another birthday.

Yes, some people do experience a change in their skin in response to seasonal weather or their skin changes when they travel to different climates, but that doesn't happen for everyone. The best you can do for skin every day of the year is to treat the concerns you have and do what maintains healthy skin.

If you experience drier skin in the winter or in a dry climate, or if the humidity in summer or in a warm climate makes your usual skin care products feel too heavy, you might need to adapt your skin care routine. But that doesn't mean you need to create an entirely new routine; it's far easier and better for your skin and budget to replace or add one or two new products to what you are already using.

Balance the needs of your skin type with the needs of your skin concerns. When we talk about skin type, we mean how oily, dry, or combination or how sensitive your skin is. Skin concerns include signs of aging, uneven skin tone, loss of firmness, clogged pores, blackheads, blemish-prone skin, redness, and sun damage from not using sunscreen daily (sunscreen is always part of the picture).

Your skin type determines the *texture* of the products you use. Whether it's a cleanser, exfoliant, moisturizer, sunscreen, or specialty formula for specific concerns (such as serums, boosters, targeted solutions, or masks), the product's texture (rich cream or lotion for dry skin and gel, lotion-gel, fluid, or liquid for normal to oily skin), again, makes all the difference in the world.

Everyone's skin needs the same fundamental ingredients, but everyone should NOT be using products with the same type of textures.

If you have dry skin, using a liquid or a matte-finish product can make your skin drier; if you have oily skin, using an emollient moisturizer will make your skin feel more oily and may potentially clog pores. This is a very straightforward concept, but many people are unaware of it. (More about all this in the next chapter.)

Know your skin care concerns. In addition to knowing your skin type (normal, oily, dry, or combination), you need to identify your specific skin care concerns to determine what types of additional specialty products you need. Balance the essential products you need (cleanser, exfoliant, sunscreen, and moisturizer) with the specialty products you need for skin concerns such as discolorations, rosacea, acne, sun damage, and advanced signs of aging. These are all pieces of the puzzle you need to put together to create the best skin care routine just for you.

Layering products is often the best way to take care of your skin. While it is possible to maintain and achieve great skin with a relatively simple skin care routine, that's only true if you have few or no multifaceted skin problems or concerns. If you are not one of the lucky few who have "normal" skin with minimal to no sun damage, then layering products with beneficial formulations specifically for your concerns is necessary to get the best results.

Sunscreen, sunscreen, sunscreen. By the end of this book you will surely be tired of hearing this, but nothing is as vital as daily sun protection. Despite the abundant research showing how damaging unprotected sun exposure is, how tanning causes irreparable harm to skin, and that sunlight is carcinogenic (tanning beds are even worse), less than 20% of the world's population wears sunscreen on a regular basis. More troubling is that far fewer know how to apply it correctly or even that wearing sunscreen and still getting a tan is devastating for skin.

Of late, sunscreen ingredients have been demonized on the internet for causing endocrine disruption and polluting the environment. We'll talk about that more later in the book, but for now, the unambiguous fact is that not applying sunscreen is deadly for your skin.

There is also the notion that sunscreen blocks the body from getting the vitamin D it needs because sun is the primary way the body makes vitamin D. While sunscreen does block vitamin D production, relying on sun exposure is a bad way to get enough vitamin D for your health. There's no reliable research showing how much sun exposure you need to obtain sufficient vitamin D for your body or how much of your body needs to be exposed. You may be shocked to learn that a tan actually blocks the skin's ability to make vitamin D, so too much exposure to the sun doesn't help either ... more about that later.

Avoid falling asleep in your makeup! For many reasons, falling asleep with your makeup on is not good for skin. Sleeping with your eye makeup on causes significant irritation that can lead to red, puffy, itchy eyes from the eyeshadow and mascara flaking and being rubbed into your eyes and the delicate skin around your eyes. When you sleep in makeup, skin looks more dull the next day because it was unable to shed/exfoliate properly at night. That can also lead to rough skin, clogged pores, and breakouts!

Packaging matters, and it bears repeating: Do not use any moisturizer, serum, booster, ` eye cream, or any skin care product containing beneficial ingredients that's packaged in a jar!

No matter how great a product's formula, jar packaging is always a deal-breaker if the product contains air-sensitive ingredients. As it turns out, almost every antioxidant and skin-restoring ingredient doesn't like air. Jar packaging repeatedly exposes these beneficial, but inherently unstable, ingredients to light and air, causing them to break down and lose their effectiveness.

Given the number and variety of products available today that come in air-reducing or airless packaging (including airless jars), why waste your money on products whose most beneficial ingredients will be less effective shortly after the first use just because it comes packaged in a pretty jar?

The neck and chest don't need different products or ingredients than the face does and there is no research anywhere in the world proving otherwise. Products labeled as being specially formulated for the neck or chest area are at the top of the list when it comes to wasting money on unnecessary products making claims that aren't true.

Regardless of the concern, from a sagging neck or the skin on your chest looking crepey, wrinkled, discolored, or dry, or if your chest, neck, or back have breakouts, the same ingredients you use to address those problems on your face are the ones that will work on your neck, chest, and back, too. This is true for sunscreens, serums, boosters, moisturizers, gentle leave-on exfoliants, and anti-acne products. Our strong recommendation is to use the same skin care routine you use for your face starting from the chest up.

Skin doesn't adapt to skin care ingredients! We've heard this one endlessly over the years, but it is physiologically impossible. Those who advocate this idea of skin adapting to ingredients are essentially saying that you're supposed to change the products you use on a regular basis—it isn't true, not even a little. This is one of the more absurd notions in skin care (okay, there are lots of absurd notions, but this one just bugs us).

Skin is the largest organ of the body and has needs similar to those of the other organs in the body. Your internal organs can no more adapt to eating healthy foods or adapt to eating unhealthy foods than your skin can adapt to the ingredients and protection it needs to be healthy.

Skin is hungry for antioxidants, skin-replenishing ingredients, and skin-restoring ingredients every day, and they never stop working. Most of them would already be present in skin if they didn't become depleted because of sun damage, pollution, and age. Skin certainly doesn't adapt to the substances it contains naturally; it just wants more of them when they start becoming depleted.

Exfoliants continue to work because skin continues to need help in shedding built-up dead skin that is constantly being generated. The same sunscreen you apply today will interrupt sun damage every time you use it for years to come. Antioxidants will always interrupt environmental damage.

This notion of your skin adapting to skin care ingredients gets confused with the fact that skin changes over time. Even the best skin care products can't stop you from getting older. They can't undo years of unprotected sun damage, prevent the eye area's fat pads from drooping and causing eyes to be baggy and puffy, stop mid-life hormonal changes from affecting skin, prevent gravity from sagging skin, or prevent other health problems along the way that change how your skin looks and feels. It's not that your skin has adapted to anything in the formulas you use; rather, your skin may need more advanced formulas or higher concentrations of key ingredients.

Believing skin adapts to skin care ingredients also gets lumped in with the science that topical antibiotics or anti-bacterial ingredients used to treat acne can eventually stop working.

But that's not about skin adapting to the antibiotic or anti-bacterial ingredient, that's about the bacteria in skin adapting and becoming resistant to that antibiotic or anti-bacterial ingredient.

CHAPTER 3

SKIN TYPE VERSUS SKIN CONCERN

WHY IS SKIN TYPE SO CONFUSING?

One of the more confusing aspects of developing an effective skin care routine is finding products that work for your skin type *and* address your skin concerns. It's important to understand the difference between skin type and skin concern. There is overlap, but there are differences that affect how you take care of your skin. Here's how it works ...

Skin type is mostly about the feel and look of your skin, meaning is it dry, oily, combination (combination refers to skin being oily in some areas, dry in others), or normal (meaning neither oily nor combination nor dry, just normal). You may also have "sensitive skin." While we feel strongly that everyone should treat their skin gently because research makes it crystal clear that harsh, irritating skin care products cause both short-term and long-term damage, those with extra sensitive skin must take extra precautionary measures with additional soothing agents and milder forms of active ingredients.

Normal skin deserves a bit more explanation: When you hear "normal" as a skin type, you might envision someone with perfect skin with minimal to no signs of dryness or oily shine, a smooth surface with no clogged pores or visible pores, and an even skin tone with no visible signs of aging and, seemingly, minimal skin care needs.

Even if you are lucky enough to have "normal" skin, the sobering fact is that it won't last if you aren't diligent about how you take care of your skin now. Eventually, someone with normal skin will have to deal with the accumulated damage from sun exposure and pollution, not to mention midlife changes that occur to skin as you move into your 40s. All those issues and more can affect your skin in ways that make it unhealthy and unbalanced.

Skin concerns include clogged pores, blackheads, uneven skin tone, dullness, breakouts, signs of aging, rough skin texture, and loss of firmness. Once you've determined what your skin type is and you know your skin concerns, you can then determine the specific products you need for your essential skin care routine. These essential products are the ones you should be using every day and, while the formulations differ based on skin type, the categories of products and core ingredients are the same for everyone.

FINDING YOUR SKIN TYPE AND CONCERNS

Lots of people are confused about their skin type and skin concerns, and we completely understand why. **The major problem we've seen over the years is that people don't realize that their skin type or skin concerns are greatly affected by the skin care products they are using or by other things they are doing to their skin, plus lifestyle choices.** All of these can end up creating a skin type or skin concern you wouldn't otherwise have.

Many things affect skin type and can cause skin concerns that wouldn't otherwise be present, such as unprotected sun exposure, diet (eating sugar, processed foods, or if you are sensitive to lactose), smoking (including secondhand smoke), pollution, and drinking too much alcohol (we love our martinis, too, but unfortunately cocktails aren't health foods). But, in addition, and high up on that list, is using skin care products that contain inflaming, irritating ingredients that cause it to react in negative ways. These types of products can make skin drier, more oily, and reddened in areas, increase the appearance of wrinkles, make skin less firm, rougher, and less radiant, trigger clogged pores, and make skin more sensitive. Sadly, non-irritating skin care products are not easy to find.

In truth, the very skin care products you are using can be a major factor in causing a skin type and/or skin concern you don't want and that you certainly don't want to become worse. You may never know your actual skin type or get your skin concerns under control if you use products that contain ingredients that cause or intensify the very problems you don't want.

If you use products that contain harsh or irritating ingredients, are too emollient or too light for your skin type, aren't gentle, or if you aren't using a sunscreen with an SPF 30 or greater, whatever feature you want to improve with your skin—it can't happen.

Products with irritating ingredients disturb and deplete skin's surface, making it drier and weakening it, which adds up to worsening signs of aging, unhealthy, dull-looking skin, and even triggering bumps, clogged pores, and blackheads. Alternatively, if you have oily skin and use overly emollient or thick-textured products, they will make it feel more oily and increase clogged pores, blackheads, or breakouts. If you use emollient moisturizers along with a drying cleanser, you can create combination skin: oily in some areas and dry in others.

If you don't use a well-formulated, gentle leave-on exfoliant, you can have an unhealthy buildup of dead surface skin that can't shed in a normal manner. This leads to dull skin with a rough, uneven texture, skin that feels less supple and firm, and skin with worsening enlarged, clogged pores, and blackheads.

If you over-scrub and use drying cleansers, regardless of your skin type, you will impair skin's surface, which will make all the problems mentioned above worse.

Until you get these external factors under control, you will find it difficult to ever really know your skin type (or have the skin type you want). The kinds of products you use make all the difference in the world when trying to reach your goal of having the best skin of your life now.

Once you've ruled out the controllable factors that can affect your skin type, it'll be much easier to determine your true skin type and to identify what your skin concerns really are. After that, you just need to find the best products to use.

HOW TO DETERMINE YOUR SKIN CONCERN(S)

In some ways this is the easiest section of the book because most of us are aware of what our skin concerns are. For example, most of us already know what fine lines, acne, clogged, enlarged pores, loss of firmness, uneven skin tone, and signs of aging look like. That's the easy part.

The most important takeaway about skin concerns is that most people have multiple skin concerns at the same time. It is not unusual for someone to have some combination of sensitive skin with red areas, fine lines, sun damage from not using a sunscreen daily, uneven skin tone, patches of dryness, and areas that are oily and have clogged pores or blackheads. This is where skin care can get complicated; once you've identified your skin concerns, then you need to add the specialty solution products to address them.

It's possible that an essential skin care routine may be enough to handle many aspects of your skin type and skin concerns. After you get the essential skin care steps down and you start to experience healthier skin, you'll be able to figure out if you need to add products to deal with stubborn or advanced skin care needs.

CREATING YOUR ESSENTIAL SKIN CARE ROUTINE

In this section, we describe how to choose and apply the best products you need to create an essential skin care routine. You can finally start having the skin you want and reveal what your skin type and skin concerns really are, not the ones you may have inadvertently imposed on it. Once you establish your essential routine, every other decision you make about your skin care routine becomes far easier (well, at least that's the goal).

Products for your essential skin care routine:

+ Cleanser
+ Gentle leave-on exfoliant
+ Daytime moisturizer with sunscreen
+ Nighttime moisturizer

Now you need to choose the skin type–appropriate texture of the product for each step:

+ Creamy, rich-textured products for dry skin
+ Light, lotion-textured products for normal skin
+ Gel-, fluid-, or watery-textured products for oily/combination skin

1. Use a gentle, water-soluble cleanser twice daily

Every morning and every night you need to cleanse your skin with the cleanser that is most appropriate for your skin type: more emollient for dry skin, more of a lotion for normal skin, and a gel or creamy lather for oily/combination skin.

Avoid pulling excessively at your skin when wiping off your makeup, as this will eventually break the skin's elastin fibers, increasing the risk of sagging. If you have to wipe off your makeup, which is usually the case if you are wearing waterproof or heavy makeup, do it with as little movement of your skin as possible!

If you want to use a **cleansing brush**, make sure the brush head is exceptionally gentle. You can also use a soft washcloth. A **scrub-type cleanser is certainly an option, BUT only if it is non-abrasive** and contains only rounded (not jagged) soft particles to provide the extra cleansing. Non-irritating is the goal for everyone.

Double cleansing (using two different cleansers or cleansing twice with the same cleanser) is an option if you wear heavy makeup, waterproof makeup, or have a need to feel extra clean. If the products you use are gentle and non-drying, this is a great option because it is very important to remove all your makeup every night.

At night, you can start or follow with a **gentle makeup remover** to be sure you've removed every bit of makeup, but again, be careful not to tug or pull at your skin.

2. Apply a leave-on exfoliant once or twice daily

The next step in your essential routine is to apply an **AHA (alpha hydroxy acid) or BHA (beta hydroxy acid) leave-on exfoliant** with a texture appropriate for your skin type. This step is important; we explain at length in the next chapter why an exfoliant is an indispensable part of any skin care routine.

3. Apply a broad-spectrum sunscreen every morning

It goes without saying, but you know we can't help ourselves: During the day, EVERY DAY, 365 days a year, rain or shine, even if you will be indoors most of the day, the last thing you put on your skin before you apply makeup is **sunscreen rated SPF 30 or greater.** Sun (daylight) damage is ever-present, and even occurs through windows. Research has shown that the damage begins within the first minute your unprotected skin sees daylight!

What is meant by "broad-spectrum"? When you see the term *broad spectrum* on a sunscreen label, it means the sunscreen was tested and confirmed to protect skin from the sun's damaging UVA rays (ultraviolet A radiation) and UVB rays (ultraviolet B radiation). UVB rays cause sunburn, while UVA rays penetrate more deeply into skin and cause cellular destruction.

Along with broad-spectrum protection, the best sunscreens for your face should also contain an array of other beneficial ingredients to fight environmental damage, restore skin's barrier, and enhance hydration so you need only one "moisturizer" in the morning, which is your moisturizing sunscreen. You shouldn't need to apply a moisturizer and then a sunscreen unless your skin is very dry. Otherwise, a brilliantly formulated facial moisturizer with sunscreen should do it all, and you should apply it to your neck, chest, hands, and arms as well if those area are not covered by clothing.

It is incredibly important to find a great sunscreen that you love to use. That means you need a sunscreen with a texture appropriate for your skin type. For someone with dry skin, a creamier formula should be perfect; for someone with normal skin, a lotion formula will be great. If you have oily or combination skin, a sheer, matte-finish sunscreen with a thin lotion or fluid texture works best (and also works beautifully under makeup).

Using a sunscreen is a necessity, but it's also important how you apply it, which makes all the difference. The key is to be sure you are getting adequate coverage. Sunscreen is probably one of the more complicated steps in skin care, but getting it right can prevent everything from signs of skin aging to skin cancer. We have a chapter just on sunscreen coming up to make sure we keep you well-informed *and* well-protected!

You can also use an eye cream, eye serum, or eye gel around your eyes for daytime, and then apply your daytime moisturizer with sunscreen over that for complete protection.

4. Apply a "moisturizer" at night
We put the word moisturizer in quotes because not everyone needs a moisturizer in the traditional sense of a lotion or cream. What's important is to give skin nourishing hydration that's brimming with antioxidants, skin-replenishing ingredients, and skin-restoring ingredients, but the way you get those ingredients on your skin varies based on your skin type.

If you have oily/combination skin, a liquid, gel, or thin serum is ideal; a lotion or cream moisturizer would be too heavy and risk clogging pores and making skin feel greasy. For dry skin, a rich emollient cream works best; for normal skin, a lotion or serum texture would be perfect.

You can also use an eye cream, eye serum, or eye gel around your eyes, but if your nighttime facial moisturizer is beautifully formulated, you can just use that around your eye area, too.

WHEN AN ESSENTIAL SKIN CARE ROUTINE ISN'T ENOUGH, YOU MAY NEED TO USE AN ADVANCED SKIN CARE ROUTINE

The building blocks for taking the best care of your skin are the essential skin care steps mentioned above. For lots of people, that's all it takes to maintain their best skin, but, as we've said, if you have other more complicated or stubborn skin problems to manage, then an essential routine will probably not be enough; that's where an advanced skin care routine is needed. An advanced routine involves layering boosters, serums, or treatment solutions for your skin concerns. These types of products can change your skin in exceptional ways. Depending on the skin type or the types of problems you need to address, these solutions can be used once or twice daily, every other day, once a week, or seasonally.

Layering is not a new concept in skin care, but given the new and advanced lightweight and highly compatible formulations, it's something those with any skin type can do without making skin (even if it's oily) feel over-loaded with products. You can get better skin once you understand how layering works and which products to use to get the best results.

WHAT'S COMING UP NEXT?

In the next chapter, we go into more detail about each step of your essential skin care routine and the types of products you should use for each step. Some of it may be repetitive, but most of you will probably find the extra details and information helpful.

CHAPTER 4

WHAT TO USE AND WHAT NOT TO USE

CLEANSERS

Cleansing the face gently yet thoroughly sets the stage for almost everything else that will take place on your skin. A great cleanser removes excess oil, dirt, impurities, sunscreen, and makeup, leaving skin smooth and fresh without feeling greasy or dry.

If you don't cleanse your skin regularly or if you don't remove all your makeup, your skin will pay the price. We're talking potential clogged pores, dry patches, puffy eyes, and red areas.

Careful, gentle cleansing and not pulling at your skin (which means wiping off makeup should be done cautiously or avoided—more about this in a bit) is the cornerstone for every skin type. Over-cleansing or using cleansers that are too drying can cause all the skin problems we mention above.

On the other hand, using a cleanser that leaves a greasy film on the face or that doesn't clean well can lead to clogged pores and dull-looking skin, and prevent moisturizers, serums, boosters, or treatment products from being absorbed and doing their job. It is essential to get this step right, and that means thoroughly, but gently, cleansing your face.

How do I choose a gentle cleanser? Generally, fragrance-free liquid or lotion-style cleansers are what you need to look for, but watch out: Some liquid and lotion cleansers can be drying and far from gentle. In short, this question is tricky to answer.

What we can say for certain is that the best cleansers, regardless of skin type, should never leave your face dry, greasy, or tight. There's a fine line between a cleanser that cleans well and one that doesn't strip vital substances from skin's surface; this is true for all skin types. Truly gentle cleansers are out there, including those from Paula's Choice Skincare.

Should you start with a makeup remover? Many people feel their cleansing routine should start with a makeup remover, such as a liquid remover, makeup wipes, or a cleansing oil. This can work well if you wear a medium- to full-coverage makeup application, waterproof makeup, or mineral-based sunscreens, but some people can get by without this extra step if they are wearing minimal makeup, so consider it optional.

Regardless of the type of makeup remover, keep in mind that wiping and pulling at the face or around the eyes is a big problem. Tugging on skin encourages sagging. The less you pull, the better your skin will hold up over the long run.

Double cleansing simply means using two different cleansers one after the other, or using the same cleanser twice, rinsing off in between. This is a great way to be sure you're removing all your makeup or if you just like an extra clean feel. The only caveat is that both cleansers must be gentle. It is never the goal for skin to feel tight, dry, "squeaky clean," or irritated.

What about facial cleansing oils? The term *facial cleansing oil* is a bit confusing because the category is not clear-cut. Some facial cleansing oils are "oils" in name only; they're more like emollient water-soluble cleansers that are meant to be rinsed off. These can be a great option if you have normal to very dry skin, or if you apply full-coverage or waterproof makeup.

Traditional facial cleansing oils typically include oil from a single plant or a blend of oils from multiple plants. The oils are massaged onto the face and then wiped off, usually with a wet washcloth or special face cloth. This is another way to remove makeup, and can be followed by a water-soluble cleanser. For those with extremely dry skin, just wiping the oil away is enough, but only if you avoid pulling and tugging at your skin as much as possible.

There are lots of myths circulating about facial cleansing oils. We prefer facts to myths, and the fact is that facial cleansing oils are not miracles for skin, they're just another option that may or may not be helpful for you depending on your skin type and concerns.

The notion that cleansing oils can somehow unclog pores by some force of chemistry that lets them pull clogs out of the pore is not supported by any research. We still don't understand the explanations we've seen for this; they defy science and physiology.

Keep in mind that many facial cleansing oils also contain fragrant oils, which present a serious problem for skin and eyes. As we repeatedly state throughout this book, essential oils and fragrance cause problems for skin. Non-fragrant plant oils are the only ones you should ever consider putting on your face.

What about bar soap? We wish we could say bar soaps are great for skin as that would make choosing a cleanser much easier and less expensive. Regrettably, that's not the case.

Bar soaps and soap-free bar cleansers tend to be too drying and irritating for the face (that can also be true for skin from the neck down). Regardless of your skin type, most bar soaps or bar cleansers present significant issues.

Many people with combination or oily skin believe that the tight sensation they feel after washing with soap means their face is really clean, but that's not the case! What you are feeling indicates that your skin was irritated, dried out, and stressed, which makes all skin problems worse. Plus, the typical ingredients that keep bar soaps and bar cleansers in their bar form can leave a film on skin that can eventually cause congested pores.

Do I need a scrub or a cleansing brush? Scrubs and cleansing brushes are certainly options as part of your daily cleansing routine, but only if they are gentle. If you want to use a scrub, be sure it does not contain any abrasive ingredients; even if they are natural, they can still tear at skin. If you want to use a cleansing brush, be sure you use only the device's "sensitive" brush head option. The brushes on such devices should feel very soft and flexible, *never* stiff or wiry before or after you start using it (some can become hard on skin after you've been using it awhile)!

You can also gently use a soft cotton washcloth with your daily cleanser. As a bonus, washcloths are far less expensive than any cleansing brush!

Scrubs, cleansing brushes, or washcloths can provide extra cleansing and can be extremely helpful in making sure you've removed all of your makeup and sunscreen at night. But, using these does not replace exfoliation; they just can't do what an effective leave-on AHA or BHA exfoliant can do.

Scrubs, cleansing brushes, and washcloths have limitations because they affect only the very top, superficial layer of skin. The way skin needs help in exfoliating the built-up layers that don't shed as they should naturally is beyond what manual exfoliation can provide. Healthy, young skin exfoliates without any help, all on its own, and it is a completely undetectable, invisible process (although the great results are definitely visible). Scrubbing skin does not, in any way, duplicate skin's natural process of exfoliation, and that process requires help as we age, mostly due to sun damage and skin disorders. That's where AHAs or BHA can step in to bring skin back to normal.

PAULA'S CHOICE SKINCARE CLEANSERS

+ **RESIST Optimal Results Hydrating Cleanser for Normal to Dry Skin**
+ **RESIST Perfectly Balanced Foaming Cleanser for Normal to Oily Skin**
+ **DEFENSE Hydrating Gel-to-Cream Cleanser for All Skin Types**
+ **SKIN BALANCING Oil-Reducing Cleanser for Normal to Oily Skin**
+ **SKIN RECOVERY Softening Cream Cleanser for Dry to Very Dry Skin**
+ **MOISTURE BOOST One Step Face Cleanser for Normal to Dry Skin**
+ **HYDRALIGHT One Step Face Cleanser for Normal to Oily Skin**

+ **CALM Nourishing Cleanser for Normal to Dry Skin**
+ **CALM Nourishing Cleanser for Normal to Oily Skin**
+ **CLEAR Pore Normalizing Cleanser for Blemish-Prone Skin**
+ **EARTH SOURCED Perfectly Natural Cleansing Gel for All Skin Types**
+ **Perfect Cleansing Oil for All Skin Types**
+ **The Unscrub for All Skin Types**
+ **Gentle Touch Makeup Remover for All Skin Types**
+ **Gentle Cleansing Cloths for All Skin Types**

TONERS: DO YOU REALLY NEED ONE?

Toners are a confusing category of skin care products. Because of misperceptions about toners, you may have read or been told not to use a toner. That's disappointing, because a well-formulated toner can provide wonderful benefits for your skin.

Toners are meant to be used after cleansing. They were once recommended to restore skin's pH balance after using a bar soap or bar cleanser because those bar cleansers can raise skin's natural pH to a level that isn't good for your skin. However, given today's gentle, water-soluble cleansers, this need has become a non-issue. (We'll talk more about the pH of skin later in the book.)

What we now know from research is that after cleansing, even if you use a gentle cleanser, your skin needs a range of ingredients to revitalize and renew its surface. A toner can instantly give skin a generous amount of the important substances we've been talking about in a way that a moisturizer cannot (lotion and cream moisturizers work differently from liquids). Plus, you really can't give your skin too much of these important reviving ingredients, including antioxidants, skin-replenishing ingredients, and skin-restoring ingredients.

The right toner can give your skin a healthy measure of what it needs to look younger, fresher, and smoother, right after cleansing and throughout the day. It also provides a bit of extra cleansing, just in case you missed some areas, such as around your hairline or jaw.

Toners for oily skin with clogged pores or breakout-prone skin: If you have oily or breakout-prone skin, you must be extremely careful when shopping for toners. That's because most toners for oily, breakout-prone skin contain irritating ingredients such as denatured or SD alcohol, witch hazel, and menthol, all of which impede skin's ability to be healthy. Using the wrong toner on oily, breakout-prone skin can cause skin to become more oily, reddened, and often dry and flaky. It's a recipe for the complaint of dry skin underneath and oily skin on top, which is sometimes referred to as dehydrated skin.

The best toners for oily or breakout-prone skin are those with ingredients that soothe and recharge skin's surface, make skin feel smoother, diminish enlarged pores, and contain antioxidants and skin-replenishing ingredients to make sure skin has what it needs to ward off dryness and sensitivity.

For combination to oily skin types, especially during summer or in warmer climates, a well-formulated toner along with a booster or serum may be the only "moisturizer" your skin needs!

Toners for dry or extra sensitive skin: Those with dry or sensitive skin typically shy away from toners because of their astringent, drying reputation; after all, the last thing dry, sensitive skin needs is harsh ingredients! But, the right toner for dry or sensitive skin can make a world of difference: You'll see less redness and flaking, and your skin will feel soothed and comfortable. The goal with toners is to quickly replenish skin after cleansing and, while that is important for all skin types, it is particularly important for those with dry or sensitive skin, as these skin types tend to have weaker barriers.

If you're skeptical (and we can't say we blame you), give a well-formulated toner a try—we know you'll be pleasantly surprised with how fast your skin improves!

Toners for combination skin: If your skin is oily on your forehead, nose, and chin and dry to normal on your cheeks or jaw area, then you have classic combination skin. Using the wrong toner on combination skin will exaggerate the dry areas and make oily areas worse (this is doubly true if breakouts and clogged pores are present).

What's the solution? You need a gentle toner with ingredients that help normalize your skin, so you'll see less dryness and less oiliness. With ongoing use as part of a complete skin care routine, you'll also see enlarged pores become smaller and the surface of skin will feel balanced and normalized.

When shopping for toners, it's critical that you consider only those that give your skin nothing but beneficial ingredients—only the good and none of the bad. Remember, great toners give back what skin needs after cleansing; bad toners take away and deplete skin's barrier.

PAULA'S CHOICE SKINCARE TONERS

+ **RESIST Advanced Replenishing Toner for Normal to Dry Skin**
+ **RESIST Weightless Advanced Repairing Toner for Normal to Oily Skin**
+ **SKIN BALANCING Pore-Reducing Toner for Normal to Oily Skin**
+ **SKIN RECOVERY Enriched Calming Toner for Dry to Very Dry Skin**
+ **HYDRALIGHT Healthy Skin Refreshing Toner for Normal to Oily Skin**
+ **MOISTURE BOOST Essential Hydrating Toner for Normal to Dry Skin**
+ **CALM Soothing Toner for Normal to Dry skin**
+ **CALM Soothing Toner for Normal to Oily Skin**
+ **EARTH SOURCED Purely Natural Refreshing Toner for All Skin Types**

WHY GENTLE LEAVE-ON EXFOLIANTS ARE SO IMPORTANT

Many people think that exfoliating skin is all about using scrubs or cleansing brushes. It turns out that both are poor options for exfoliation because they are limited in reach. Even the best scrubs and cleansing brushes (meaning they are gentle and don't tear at skin) can clean only the very surface of skin. Cleansing is not the same as exfoliating; exfoliation goes below the surface, beyond where scrubs and cleansing brushes can go.

What *can* reach those built-up layers without disturbing or tearing at the surface of skin are well-formulated AHA (alpha hydroxy acids, such as glycolic acid and lactic acid) and BHA (beta hydroxy acid, which is only salicylic acid) leave-on exfoliants. Scrubs and cleansing brushes can't do a fraction of what AHAs and BHA can do; they not only gently exfoliate skin, but also increase hydration (yes, leave-on exfoliants are brilliant at increasing hydration), as well as reinforce, strengthen, and soften skin. No scrub or cleansing brush can do that.

Without question, almost everyone can benefit from daily use of a well-formulated leave-on AHA or BHA exfoliant. A gentle leave-on exfoliant helps the turnover (shedding) of dead layers of skin when it can't do it naturally on its own any longer.

This completely non-abrasive form of exfoliation not only has the benefits mentioned above, but also improves signs of aging, uneven skin tone, dullness, and breakouts (it is amazing for acne); dramatically reduces clogged pores and pore size; and fades all colors of post-acne marks. Don't let the "acid" in the name of these amazing ingredients scare you, especially considering that our skin's surface is naturally acidic.

Here's why AHAs or BHA are so important: When we're young, skin naturally sheds immense amounts of dead cells every day, but this shedding process slows and can practically stop due to years of sun damage, dry skin, oily skin, midlife changes, and various other skin concerns. All of those things can lead to a buildup of dead skin on and below the surface of skin and inside the pore lining. The result is dull, dry, or flaky skin, clogged, enlarged pores, white bumps, magnified fine lines, rough texture, loss of firmness, and uneven skin tone.

Adding a gentle leave-on exfoliant to your skin care routine puts everything in balance again by helping skin exfoliate like it did when we were younger. You can't feel what it's doing, and you won't see flaking skin, but the appearance of your skin will be better overnight.

What is the difference between an AHA exfoliant and a BHA exfoliant? The answer is a bit complicated because when properly formulated, both AHAs and BHA are brilliant options for exfoliating the surface of skin and both can work for similar skin types and concerns. Despite their similarities, however, there are distinct advantages to each that will help you decide which one is right for you or whether you should experiment with both.

AHAs, in concentrations between 5% and 10%, are preferred for those whose chief concern is dry skin because AHAs do not penetrate easily through oil, so they are less compatible for those who have oily/combination skin or clogged pores. Generally, lower concentrations are preferred for maintenance and higher concentrations for advanced signs of aging and sun damage. The AHAs with the most research behind them are glycolic acid and lactic acid, but there is some research showing that polyhydroxy acids, malic acid, mandelic acid, and tartaric acid also provide benefits.

BHA, in concentrations between 0.5% and 9%, is preferred for oily skin, clogged pores, blackheads, enlarged pores, and breakouts because BHA (salicylic acid) can penetrate through and help normalize the oil that's clogging your pores. This oil gridlock plays a role in preventing skin from shedding normally. A well-formulated BHA exfoliant helps stabilize the pore lining and improve its shape, allowing for a more normal flow of oil out of the pore, significantly lessening breakouts. BHA also has anti-inflammatory properties that AHAs don't, so BHA is great for sensitive or redness-prone skin. Lower concentrations are preferred for maintenance, higher concentrations are ideal for stubborn acne-clogged pores, blackheads, and white bumps.

Some products contain a mix of AHAs and BHA, an interesting option for certain skin types. Some people even like to alternate the use of different AHA and BHA products, using one in the morning and the other at night.

To get the most benefit from your AHA or BHA exfoliant, experiment with different strengths to see which concentration gives you the best results.

Apply an AHA or BHA product once or twice per day, depending on your skin type and skin concerns. Those with advanced problems will probably require twice-daily application, while others can benefit from one application per day or every other day. Advanced skin problems will benefit from regular use of products with higher concentration of AHAs or BHA. Again, experimenting is the best way to determine how often and what concentration works best for you.

Both AHA and BHA exfoliants can be used around the eye area, but not on the eyelid or directly under the eye (along the lower lash line). They also work great for lines around the edge of the mouth, but just the edge; don't put them directly on your lips!

Apply the AHA or BHA product on your face after cleansing and toning.

Once you've applied your exfoliant, you can immediately apply any other product in your routine, such as moisturizer, serum, eye cream, sunscreen, and/or foundation. But, don't forget, sunscreen is always the last skin care product you apply during the day.

Finding the right concentration of AHA or BHA is important. Higher concentrations are needed when you have stubborn or advanced skin concerns; lower concentrations are best when you only need to help your skin behave normally.

Finding the product with the best *texture* for your skin type is also useful. For normal to dry skin, a lotion, serum, or cream is best; for normal to oily skin, a liquid or gel texture will make your skin very happy.

Our suggestion is to get started by choosing an AHA or BHA exfoliant based on the information above and carefully noting the results you get over a period of a few weeks. You can always experiment by purchasing a higher or lower strength version or by adding another exfoliant and alternating (a lower strength in the morning, a higher strength at night). Again, it all depends on how stubborn or advanced your skin concerns are and how your skin responds to the products you use.

PAULA'S CHOICE SKINCARE AHA PRODUCTS

+ **SKIN PERFECTING 8% AHA Gel for All Skin Types**
+ **SKIN PERFECTING 8% AHA Lotion for All Skin Types**
+ **RESIST Daily Smoothing Treatment with 5% AHA for Normal to Dry Skin**
+ **RESIST Advanced Smoothing Treatment with 10% AHA for All Skin Types**
+ **SKIN REVEALING Body Lotion with 10% AHA for All Skin Types**

PAULA'S CHOICE SKINCARE BHA PRODUCTS

+ **SKIN PERFECTING 2% BHA Liquid Exfoliant for Normal to Oily Skin**
+ **SKIN PERFECTING 2% BHA Gel Exfoliant for Normal to Oily Skin**
+ **SKIN PERFECTING 2% BHA Lotion Exfoliant for Normal to Dry Skin**
+ **CALM 1% BHA Lotion Exfoliant for All Skin Types**
+ **RESIST Daily Pore-Refining Treatment with 2% BHA for Normal to Oily Skin**
+ **RESIST Advanced Pore-Refining Treatment 4% BHA for Normal to Oily Skin**
+ **BHA 9 Treatment for All Skin Types**
+ **CLEAR Regular Strength Anti-Redness Exfoliating Solution with 2% BHA for Blemish-Prone Skin**
+ **CLEAR Extra Strength Anti-Redness Exfoliating Solution with 2% BHA for Blemish-Prone Skin**
+ **CLEAR Acne Body Spray for Blemish-Prone Skin**
+ **Weightless Body Treatment with 2% BHA for All Skin Types**

DOES EVERYONE NEED TO APPLY A MOISTURIZER?

Whether it's called a moisturizer, wrinkle cream, firming cream, anti-aging cream, or something else (the variations are endless), a moisturizer is supposed to improve skin's softness, smoothness, and ability to hold onto the vital substances it needs to look and feel younger; give skin what it needs to protect itself—to the extent possible—from pollution and environmental damage; and replenish skin with the natural substances it can't make anymore because of sun damage and/or age. Some moisturizers are brilliant at this, but a surprising number of them fall far short. Notably, that shortcoming applies to many of the more expensive options.

Although the standard term for this skin care step is "moisturizer," it's not literally about giving skin moisture (meaning water), and it isn't about applying a lotion or cream. This means that not everyone needs a moisturizer, at least not what we think of as a traditional "moisturizer" that comes in a lotion or cream form to be applied twice a day.

Instead, what everyone needs twice daily is to give skin ample amounts of antioxidants, skin-restoring ingredients, and skin-replenishing ingredients that balance and maintain skin's natural water levels (which vary as skin moves cells from the lower layers of skin to the surface). Those amazing ingredients don't need to be in a lotion or cream! This is especially important to know if you have oily, combination, or breakout-prone skin because, as you likely know, creams and lotions often make those issues worse.

Regardless of the product name or texture, a product loaded with these types of ingredients is vital for making skin look as young and healthy as possible and for maintaining hydration. Ironically, if giving skin water was all it took to not have dry skin, a shower or bath would be all you'd need. But, soaking in a tub or taking long showers does just the opposite: It breaks down skin's barrier and causes water *loss*!

When a "moisturizer" is well-formulated and includes an array of beneficial ingredients, the only thing you need to consider is the texture of the product. If they are well-formulated, the only thing that differentiates "moisturizers" or anti-wrinkle products are their textures, not their name.

If you have dry to very dry skin, you need a "moisturizer" with a creamy or balm-like texture; if you have normal to dry skin, a lotion or light cream-gel formula will work well. If you have normal to slightly dry skin or combination skin, a lightweight lotion, water-based gel, or thin fluid is your best choice. If you have oily skin and clogged pores, a sheer gel, fluid, or liquid "moisturizer" is the absolute best option.

PAULA'S CHOICE SKINCARE MOISTURIZERS FOR NORMAL TO DRY SKIN

+ **RESIST Barrier Repair Moisturizer with Retinol for Normal to Dry Skin**
+ **RESIST Intensive Repair Cream with Retinol for Dry to Very Dry Skin**
+ **CLINICAL Ultra-Rich Moisturizer for Dry to Very Dry Skin**
+ **SKIN RECOVERY Replenishing Moisturizer for Normal to Dry Skin**
+ **CALM Restoring Moisturizer for Normal to Dry Skin**
+ **Omega + Complex Moisturizer for Normal to Dry Skin**
+ **MOISTURE BOOST Hydrating Treatment Cream for Normal to Dry Skin**

PAULA'S CHOICE SKINCARE MOISTURIZERS FOR NORMAL TO OILY SKIN

+ **RESIST Anti-Aging Clear Skin Hydrator for Normal to Oily Skin**
+ **CALM Restoring Moisturizer for Normal to Oily Skin**
+ **SKIN BALANCING Invisible Finish Moisture Gel for Normal to Oily Skin**
+ **HYDRALIGHT Moisture-Infusing Lotion for Normal to Oily Skin**
+ **CLEAR Oil-Free Moisturizer for Normal to Oily Skin**

PAULA'S CHOICE SKINCARE MOISTURIZERS FOR ALL SKIN TYPES

+ **CLINICAL Ceramide-Enriched Firming Moisturizer for All Skin Types**
+ **DEFENSE Nightly Reconditioning Moisturizer for All Skin Types**
+ **EARTH SOURCED Antioxidant Enriched Natural Moisturizer for All Skin Types**
+ **Water-Infusing Electrolyte Moisturizer for All Skin Types**
+ **Probiotic Nutrient Moisturizer for All Skin Types**
+ **CBD Skin Transformative Treatment Milk for All Skin Types**

SUNSCREEN, SUNSCREEN, SUNSCREEN!

It's okay to be obsessive about some things, like eating healthy, brushing your teeth, driving safely, and using sunscreen, SPF 30 or greater, 365 days a year, rain or shine, on every part of your face and body that will be exposed to daylight. Daily application of a moisturizer with SPF 30 or greater (or foundation with SPF 30 or greater) is mandatory if you're ever going to have the best skin of your life.

If you are dedicated to applying sunscreen every day you'll have younger, healthier looking skin longer than you could possibly ever have without applying it regularly. There is no debate in the scientific literature that **sunscreen is the #1 anti-aging skin care product you can use.** Unprotected exposure to ultraviolet (UV) light is, according to most experts, the primary cause of virtually every sign of skin aging.

Sunscreen is the cornerstone of a skin care routine because without it, nothing else you do to improve the youthfulness, health, and appearance of your skin will have enduring impact. UV exposure without protection literally, steadily, and cumulatively destroys skin, and even the best skin care formulations can't keep up with that ongoing damage.

No matter what you've been told, the fact is that the only real difference between a nighttime moisturizer and a daytime moisturizer is sunscreen. All the other ingredients that skin needs (antioxidants, skin-replenishing ingredients, and skin-restoring ingredients) also should be included in moisturizers with sunscreen.

Beyond providing protection of SPF 30 or greater, your daytime moisturizer should contain an array of beneficial ingredients similar to that in your nighttime moisturizer. And, as we mentioned, there is no research showing that skin needs different ingredients during the night versus during the day. Whatever you've heard to the contrary is not backed up by science.

The texture issue also applies for your daytime moisturizer with sunscreen. If you have dry skin, an emollient cream moisturizer with SPF works best. If you have more normal skin, a light lotion texture is perfect. If you have normal to oily or combination skin, a very light, fluid texture with a soft matte finish is ideal.

We discuss sunscreens more in the next chapter to address the controversies surrounding their safety and environmental impact. We also list Paula's Choice Skincare's moisturizers with sunscreens in that chapter.

EYE CREAMS AND GELS

A separate product labeled as being for the eye area is an option as long as it's a well-formulated product containing ingredients that are helpful for skin around the eyes. We know that sounds like a no-brainer, but there are lots of eye creams that contain ingredients that are not suitable for skin anywhere around the eyes (or elsewhere on the face).

All the marketing hype about how eye creams are specially formulated for the sensitive, thin skin around the eyes or that they get rid of puffy eyes, dark circles, and lift or tighten sagging skin any better than a facial product just isn't true. There are some ingredients considered special for the eye area, but, for the most part, the same essential ingredients that benefit facial skin also benefit skin in the eye area. It's perfectly fine to use a great facial moisturizer in the eye area, which is why we often say that not everyone needs an "eye" cream (or "eye" gel or "eye" serum), but using one is fine if it's loaded with beneficial ingredients and is non-irritating.

The major reason you would not want to use your facial moisturizer around the eye area is if the skin in the eye area is different from the skin on the rest of your face.

For example, if the skin around your eyes is drier than the skin on your face, you'll need to use a more emollient moisturizer around the eyes. This also might be true if the skin on your face is oily, in which case, the gel or liquid moisturizing formula that works great on the oily or combination areas of your face would probably not be moisturizing enough for the eye area, which can tend to be dry. But again, that product doesn't have to be labeled "eye" cream.

When all is said and done, if it makes you feel better to use a product that is labeled as being special for the eye area, as many people do, that's fine; if it's a great product, we couldn't be happier.

Something you must keep in mind for the eye area is sun protection, but it turns out that most products labeled as eye creams, eye gels, or eye serums do not provide sun protection. Because sun protection is as critically important for the eye area as it is for the rest of your face, be sure to apply your facial sunscreen (either a lotion or cream or foundation) with SPF 30 or greater over your eye cream every day, rain or shine. Your mantra is: Eyes need SPF too!

Speaking of sunscreens for the eye area, we strongly recommend using only mineral-based sunscreen formulas around the eyes. "Mineral" means that they contain titanium dioxide and/or zinc oxide as the only active ingredients. Both of these naturally derived active ingredients are exceptionally gentle, which is very important for the eye area. It's not that synthetic sunscreen ingredients aren't effective, because they are, it's just that they aren't as gentle as mineral-based sunscreen ingredients.

We'll talk more about what works for dark circles and puffy eyes later in the book because all eye products—even the best ones—have limitations. We're all about truth in beauty and you need to know what those limitations are.

PAULA'S CHOICE SKINCARE PRODUCTS DESIGNED FOR THE EYE AREA

+ **CLINICAL Ceramide-Enriched Firming Eye Cream**
+ **RESIST Anti-Aging Eye Gel**
+ **RESIST Anti-Aging Eye Cream**
+ **Omega + Complex Eye Cream**

DO YOU NEED TO USE A FACIAL MASK?

The answer is: No. Of all the skin care products you need to be applying on a regular basis, a mask is truly optional. The best ones assuredly can provide benefits, but masks are more enjoyable than they are essential for having great skin.

The bigger issue is that lots of masks are poorly formulated, many containing essential oils and other potentially irritating ingredients. We think companies include such ingredients so your face tingles when you put the mask on, so you psychologically feel that it's having an effect. But, tingling is not good for skin; it absolutely does not mean the mask is working. Rather, the tingling sensation means skin-damaging irritation is taking place.

One more point: The expectations of what masks can do are often unrealistic, especially when it comes to detoxing skin (we explain that later in the book, too). Watch out for face masks that claim to be cure-alls for a long list of skin woes. Using a mask instead of the critical skin care products you use daily, such as leave-on exfoliants, sunscreens, and products brimming with antioxidants, is not a worthwhile trade-off.

Having said that, if you love masking, there are some brilliant face mask formulas available, and those are the ones you should use (by now, you have a really good idea of what the important skin care ingredients are and what ones to avoid). Following is an overview of the different mask categories to consider based on the research of what they can and cannot do for skin.

Charcoal masks and clay masks can be helpful for oily skin because they have unique absorbent properties and a relatively gentle drawing action that helps dislodge surface debris from over-filled pores.

A well-formulated charcoal mask or clay mask will leave your skin shine-free, but not dried out. These types of masks can feel temporarily "tightening," but they should not leave skin uncomfortably taut or be difficult to rinse. Unfortunately, most charcoal or clay masks also include irritating ingredients, ranging from menthol to denatured or SD alcohol, lemon, eucalyptus, mint, and essential oils. Stay away from those ingredients and you'll do fine.

Peel-off masks can help gently remove a superficial layer of gunk from pores and a thin layer of dead surface skin without any problem. These masks also immediately create a nice, smooth look and feel on skin. The downside is that many peel-off masks contain irritating ingredients and some adhere too strongly to skin, so pulling them off takes effort and stretches skin. Some hard-to-remove peel-off masks can damage the barrier of skin by literally stripping off too much of it, leaving skin weakened and irritated.

What we are most worried about are the homemade peel-off charcoal mask recipes we've seen (sometimes called "blackhead" masks). Most of them are downright scary for skin because they include an adhesive base made with glue, or even worse, *superglue*! Yes, we said superglue, and as you can well imagine, this is terribly harmful to skin. Check out the videos people have posted showing how painful they are to pull off. Please, do not try this at home!

Skin-brightening masks are intended to improve the appearance of uneven skin tone and to bring radiance to a dull complexion. The best of them include concentrated combinations of effective brightening ingredients, such as arbutin, licorice, bearberry, and niacinamide, and many are formulated so you can sleep in them. Doing so is even better because it gives the good ingredients more time to absorb and deliver the most benefit. There are no downsides to skin-brightening masks as long as they are free of any kind of skin-sensitizing ingredients!

Sheet masks started as part of a Korean (K-Beauty) skin care craze that spread all over the world. These fiber, rubber, gel, bamboo, or cloth-like masks are saturated with skin care ingredients that you're supposed to leave on your face for a rather long period of time (some recommend between 20 and 40 minutes every day), with the claim that the sheet mask itself allows the ingredients to penetrate better than other types of masks. Regrettably, that claim isn't true. Sheet masks do not help ingredients absorb better.

Ingredients' absorption into skin is based primarily on their molecular size, and sheet masks don't change that no matter what they're made of. Even if sheet masks could help ingredients penetrate better, you don't need every ingredient to be absorbed the same. Some ingredients need to remain on the surface, others to absorb a bit more, and others to absorb deeper.

There are a few studies showing that sheet masks can increase hydration, but none of those studies compared the increase in hydration with that of just using a moisturizer, lotion, serum, or booster. Why waste your precious time using a sheet mask when other leave-on products—including overnight masks—work far better, faster, and don't require waiting around?

One other thing about sheet masks: They tend to be messy, are dramatically less cost-effective per use than regular facial masks, and add excess waste to the environment. Moreover, there isn't any research showing that the delivery system has any advantages over that of traditional masks.

Sleep masks are meant to be left on overnight to lock in hydration and add anti-aging benefits (depending on the formula). Of all the mask categories out there, this one makes the most sense. Keeping beneficial ingredients on skin longer than a traditional, rinse-off mask means the ingredients in the sleep masks have more time to work, making them more effective. We've seen several such masks that contain an impressive array of super-hydrating ingredients, making them a nice add-on for times when your skin feels extra dry or dehydrated. Sleep masks can be applied in place of or on top of your regular nighttime moisturizer.

Do it yourself (DIY) face masks are meant to turn your pantry and refrigerator into your own skin care lab by following an assortment of recipes, which can include everything from honey to coconut oil, turmeric, yogurt, oatmeal, avocados, vinegar, lemon, grapefruit, tea, baking soda, mayonnaise, eggs, and lots of other food-based ingredients.

These concoctions claim to be good for everything from acne to wrinkles. Homemade masks are tempting because they're as natural as you can get (which is important to a lot of people) and they're inexpensive. But, does inexpensive and natural add up to good skin care? It all depends on which ingredients you're combining and what you're trying to improve about your skin. If you're using non-fragrant plant oils for your dry skin, that's probably the best DIY recipe to consider, but almost all the other DIY recipes we've seen contain irritating ingredients that are not good for anyone's skin.

Bubble masks are as gimmicky as it gets. We say gimmicky because the "bubble" effect has zero skin benefit. Typically, bubble masks have a gel-like texture that morphs into a bubbling foam due to a mixture of solvents and perfluorocarbons (neither of which is good for skin) in the formula. The worst bubble masks also include ingredients that make your skin tingle so you think they're doing something, but that tingling is actually your skin telling you it's being irritated. We're all for masks being fun to use, but not if the formula poses risks to skin or is void of benefits beyond a cool chemistry trick.

PAULA'S CHOICE SKINCARE MASKS

+ **RADIANCE Renewal Mask for All Skin Types**
+ **Super Hydrate Overnight Mask for All Skin Types**
+ **Rehydrating Moisture Mask for Normal to Dry Skin**
+ **SKIN RECOVERY Hydrating Treatment Mask for Normal to Dry Skin**
+ **SKIN BALANCING Oil-Absorbing Mask for Normal to Oily Skin**
+ **Pore Clarifying Charcoal Gel Mask for Normal to Oily Skin**
+ **CLEAR Purifying Clay Mask for Blemish-Prone Skin**

DO YOU NEED TO USE PH-BALANCED PRODUCTS?

Many topics in skin care are complicated, and this is one of them. How the pH of skin relates to the products we use is indeed interesting. Finding pH-balanced skin care products is easier than you might have been led to believe. It's a myth that your skin care products must have an exact pH number to be good for your skin. Here are the facts about skin and pH.

We'll start with a bit of science. The term "pH" is an acronym for "potential of hydrogen," which indicates how acidic or alkaline a substance is. The pH of a solution is indicated by numbers that range from 0 to 14. A pH of 7 is neutral; anything below 7 is considered acidic, and anything above 7 is considered alkaline. Lemon juice has a pH of 2 (very acidic), ammonia has a pH of 12 (highly alkaline), and tap water typically has a pH of 7. Skin also has a pH value, although the research doesn't always agree on what that number is. Generally, skin's pH is between 4.7 to 5.5, which makes it fairly acidic.

The concept of using pH-balanced products is based on the notion that you should only apply products that match the natural pH of your skin so as not to disrupt it. When skin's pH is left undisturbed (referred to as skin's **acid mantle**), it plays an important role in maintaining the structure of skin and protecting it from the environment.

Skin's acid mantle also plays a role in balancing skin's microbiome (the balance of probiotics—good and bad bacteria and other microbes on skin), which is essential for skin health. An acidic microbiome makes it difficult for harmful bacteria to grow but lets the good bacteria flourish. An alkaline microbiome does just the opposite.

Repeatedly disturbing skin's pH by making it either too alkaline or too acidic can cause lots of problems, which is why it makes sense to use products that don't disturb skin's natural pH balance. There is some confusion about this, as some people interpret it to mean they should only use products that have the same pH range as their skin—that just isn't realistic.

First, it's impossible to know a product's pH at a glance when shopping because most labels do not specify the pH. More importantly, you don't need to be concerned about the pH level of your products because the vast majority of both rinse-off and leave-on skin care products are already pH-balanced!

Now the question becomes: What is meant by a product being pH-balanced? By some standards, a pH-balanced product is supposed to match skin's normal pH. It might not sound like a big deal for skin to have a pH range of 4.7 to 5.5, but from a scientific perspective, that is a fairly broad range. In other words, not everyone's skin has the same pH, so what is pH-balanced for you is not necessarily going to be pH-balanced for me.

Research also shows that the mild disruptions to skin's pH, from using an AHA or BHA leave-on exfoliant (whose pH should be between 3 and 4 to be effective), a mineral-based sunscreen with a pH of 7.5, or getting your face wet with water (pH of 7), have only a temporary effect. The skin naturally equalizes to its normal pH pretty quickly, as long as you don't go to extremes (by extremes, we mean products with a pH of less than 3 or greater than 8). Research shows that using products that have such extreme pH values causes a more significant disruption to skin's pH, so it takes skin longer to get back to normal.

During this extended time to return to normalcy, skin is vulnerable to factors that can trigger breakouts, signs of eczema, redness, and sensitivity. That's why daily use of products whose pH is too high or too low can visibly and progressively damage skin.

We're often asked if it's OK to immediately layer products that have different pH levels, such as applying a moisturizer (usually a pH range of 5 to 6) over an AHA or BHA exfoliant (pH range of 3 to 4). People worry that doing might cause one or both products to not work because the different pH levels cause the products to conflict. This concern about their interaction means that many people wait 20 minutes or more before applying another skin care product—you absolutely do not have to wait!

The reason you don't have to wait is because once the pH range of a water-based product is established, it will hold within that range even when applied at the same time as products outside that pH range. That's because the ingredients that chemists use to establish a product's pH range are strong enough to keep it within the desired range no matter what you apply at the same time.

It's far easier to disrupt the pH of your skin than it is to disrupt the pH of a skin care product. To move the product's pH out of its range or to have it significantly alter the pH of other products, you'd need to add a lot of water, heat, and time (we're talking several days).

Recently, there have been concerns that washing with regular tap water can disrupt skin's pH, and that you should wash with sparkling water instead. The issue is based on the fact that tap water has a pH of around 7, sometimes higher depending on the mineral content of the water in your neighborhood. Such pH numbers are perceived as being too high for skin's natural acid mantle, with a pH of 4.7 to 5.5. The claim is that because carbonated or sparkling water has a pH of 5.5, it's more compatible with skin.

That may sound reasonable at first, but it ends up being a mix of bad science and misinformation. First, most sparkling water does not have a pH of 5.5, rather its pH is between 3 and 4; even if sparkling water had a pH of 5.5, that's still higher than most people's natural pH. Second, a neutral pH of 7 (which is what tap water typically has) is not considered disruptive of skin's natural pH. It's fine to wash your skin with plain, old tap water!

CHAPTER 5

SUN DAMAGE AND SUNSCREEN

SUN DAMAGE IS A SERIOUS PROBLEM

Sun protection is so important it merits its own chapter and us repeating as often as we can: Daily exposure to daylight (which comes through clouds, rain, and windows) without protection is one of the worst things you can do to your skin. Research makes it clear that repeated, unprotected sun exposure, getting sunburned, repeatedly getting a tan, or, even worse, using a tanning bed on a regular basis, causes irreparable damage. Over the years, in the absence of sun protection and sun-smart behavior, sun exposure wreaks havoc on your skin.

Sun damage isn't only a threat when the sun is shining; it's also a threat whenever and wherever you see daylight. And the **damage starts happening the first minute your unprotected skin sees daylight**! That research, from years ago, shocked even us, but it also changed how we deal with sun protection. Hopefully, it will change how you deal with it, too.

Years of unprotected sun exposure or getting a tan puts your skin on the fast track to premature aging and the risk of skin cancer.

Signs of aging caused by unprotected sun exposure include fine lines, discolorations, sagging, uneven skin tone, texture changes, dullness, and large pores. And all of these signs will be apparent far sooner for those who aren't diligent about protecting their skin from daylight. Dermatologists are seeing younger and younger people with skin cancer and visible signs of premature aging than ever before.

The problem is that the topic of sunscreens and all the details surrounding their use has become a confusing mess of incomplete or misleading information—which is what this chapter aims to sort out!

SUN DAMAGE AND ENLARGED PORES

It isn't common knowledge that unprotected sun exposure can cause large pores. Most people think enlarged pores are just related to oily skin, clogged pores, or genetics, but those aren't the only causes. The truth, according to the research, is that the more sun damage you have, the less firm your skin will be over time, which causes sagging. As the skin sags, it takes the pore with it, and the stretching actually makes the pore larger. In addition, when any amount of oil is present in the pore, unprotected sun exposure increases free radical damage directly inside the pore; an extremely problematic, yet fascinating, phenomenon that results in impaired pores that become larger over time.

HOW AND WHEN YOU APPLY SUNSCREEN IS IMPORTANT!

Using a daytime moisturizer with sunscreen and knowing how to apply it is a complicated, confusing, and controversial issue. We certainly understand if you're wondering what to do. Aside from application, what always confuses people are the directions to reapply sunscreen every two hours! That seems ridiculously inconvenient, to say the least. If you're wearing makeup, are you supposed to wash it all off, reapply sunscreen, and then redo your makeup every two hours throughout the day? Who has time for all that?!

Then there's the issue of vitamin D and whether or not sunscreen ingredients are safe. These are all valid concerns when it comes to sunscreen, and we're here to help you weigh the pros and cons so you can make the best decision for your skin. It's not an exaggeration to say your skin's life depends on it.

We'll start with the SPF rating on sunscreens (which is not an easy concept):

+ "SPF" stands for **S**un **P**rotection **F**actor, a sunscreen rating system that comes with a number, such as SPF 30. The SPF number indicates the length of time your skin can be exposed to sunlight without turning pink (meaning your skin will start burning) when wearing that product. The SPF number reflects only time.

+ The SPF rating is a mathematical equation that is difficult for many people to understand, but understanding it is essential if you want to be sure you're getting the protection you need:

  1. First, you need to know how many minutes it typically takes for your skin to turn pink without sun protection.

  2. If in the past your skin normally started to turn pink after 15 minutes of unprotected sun exposure (something you should never do, but most people have experienced this), then that 15 minutes is your baseline. You multiply that number of minutes by the SPF rating on the sunscreen. That's how long the product will provide sun protection.

  3. This is what the math looks like: The sunscreen you want to use has an SPF 30. You multiply that number by the number of minutes you can be in the sun without your skin

turning pink. In this example, we're using 15 minutes for how long you can stay in the sun without turning pink.

4. Here's the equation: SPF 30 × 15 minutes = 450 minutes = 7.5 hours. That's how long the sunscreen should offer sun protection if you apply it correctly (meaning liberally) and if you're not swimming or sweating.

+ Although using a product rated SPF 15 will get you an SPF 15 level of protection, research over the past several years has shown that an SPF 15 product does not provide adequate protection. More recent research has revealed that SPF 30 or greater is critical to getting the daily protection you need. Medical boards around the world have almost unanimously agreed with this.

+ The two types of ultraviolet (UV) rays (invisible radiation from the sun) that damage skin are UVA and UVB. UVA rays are more dangerous because they are the sun's silent killers. You don't feel them, they don't cause sunburn, they penetrate through windows, and they absorb deeper into skin, causing cell mutations. UVB rays cause sunburn and, therefore, can cause severe burns in a short period of time. UVB rays are strongest in sunny climates between the hours of 10:00 a.m. and 2:00 p.m.; UVA rays maintain a relatively consistent intensity during daylight hours throughout the entire year. A sunscreen labeled "broad-spectrum" must contain ingredients proven to protect skin from both types of UV rays.

+ You must apply sunscreen liberally to get the benefit of the SPF number on the label. Unfortunately, most people don't apply sunscreen liberally, which is detrimental to their skin. This common mistake might lead you to believe that the sunscreen you applied isn't effective because you think the sheer layer you applied has you protected, when it doesn't. If you're getting even a little bit of a tan or seeing brown spots showing up on your skin, you are not applying sunscreen adequately (or not reapplying as often as necessary for longer days outdoors).

+ You must apply sunscreen before you leave the house. Do not wait until you get to your destination to apply it—that is a huge skin care mistake. A lot of damage can take place from the time you leave your house until you get to your destination. Remember, **sun damage begins within the first minute your unprotected skin sees daylight.**

Does the sunscreen you applied in the morning still work in the late afternoon, following a day at the office or at school? The answer is, yes, it still works, but its effectiveness depends on how much time you spend outdoors. That's because the sunscreen's active ingredients break down in response to direct exposure to daylight, not in response to the passage of time during a single day.

On an average day (if you're in an office or otherwise indoors), your morning application of sunscreen is still going to provide enough UV protection on your way home, assuming you applied a liberal amount of a broad-spectrum SPF 30 (or greater) product in the morning.

If you're sweating or swimming, you must use water-resistant sunscreen and follow the instructions for reapplication exactly as described on the label.

Sunscreen is the last product you apply to your skin before applying your makeup or getting dressed. You don't want to dilute its effectiveness.

As we mentioned at the start of this chapter, for regular sunscreen use, most sunscreens have directions telling you to reapply the sunscreen every two hours, which is completely impractical if you're wearing makeup. This recommendation to reapply sunscreen every two hours is based on the following:

Most people don't apply sunscreen liberally enough, which means you won't be getting the SPF protection shown on the label. If you do not apply sunscreen liberally, then the apply-every-two-hours guideline makes sense, regardless of how inconvenient it may be when you're wearing makeup. The thinking goes like this: If you aren't good about applying sunscreen liberally, then reapplying every two hours after direct daylight exposure will add up to liberal application because of the extra layers of sunscreen you're putting on; this also compensates for the sunscreen's losing its effectiveness with ongoing exposure to UV light (this is a natural part of how current sunscreens work).

How much to apply: There are many measurements given to help you figure out how much sunscreen to use, but how much to use depends completely on the area you're covering. What we suggest is to smooth a layer of sunscreen you can see over skin that will be exposed to the sun, and then gently massage it into skin until absorbed. Then add a little more or layer another sunscreen product over it (yes, we love to layer different sunscreen products to ensure we're getting liberal application, as long as each one is rated SPF 30 or greater). We understand that it may feel a bit unpleasant until it absorbs, but the protection it affords is worth this temporary feeling. Don't forget your chest, arms, ears, and hands (and any other areas of exposed skin)!

How often to apply: Aside from everyday use (no exceptions), a single liberal application each morning of a product rated SPF 30 or greater will keep you protected for a normal workday (indoors), a walk to lunch, and the drive home. If you spend more than three or four hours in direct sunlight during the day, it's a good idea to reapply your sunscreen—and, yes, that means redoing your makeup, which is why we advise touching up with a pressed or loose powder rated SPF 30 or greater. (Please don't shoot the messenger, we're just giving you the facts—mostly what we want you to do is wear sunscreen; just that step alone is better than nothing at all.)

If you're sweating or swimming, you must reapply your sunscreen regardless of the SPF number on the product. If the sunscreen is labeled "very water-resistant," you get about 80 minutes of protection after skin gets wet. If the label states "water-resistant," you get only about 40 minutes of protection after you get wet. But don't forget, even if you use those types of sunscreens, you'll be rubbing them off when towel drying, so in that scenario, you must be sure to reapply. No sunscreen is ever waterproof or sweatproof, so you must follow the directions and reapply regardless of any claims to the contrary.

When washing or sanitizing your hands, you must reapply your sunscreen immediately afterward because the cleansing ingredients remove the sunscreen.

Getting any amount of a tan (except from a self-tanner) is damaging to skin. Putting sunscreen on, even a sunscreen with a very high SPF, and then basking in the sun to develop a tan is the absolute opposite of being sun-smart. Despite how healthy some people think getting a tan may look, tanning even a little is a damage response and a very bad thing for skin.

It's also critical to understand that being indoors doesn't mean your skin is protected from sun exposure. If you're sitting next to a window, you won't get sunburned because windows protect you from UVB rays (the rays that cause sunburn); however, unless the window has special UVA shielding, your skin will NOT be protected from the sun's UVA rays. These rays absolutely get through windows. This is one factor you must take into consideration when deciding when and how often to reapply your sunscreen. Staying indoors during the day does not protect your skin if you are near windows.

When should you apply sunscreen? Every day, as the last step in your skin care routine before you apply your makeup and on areas of your body that will be exposed to UV light (do this before you get dressed). **Sunscreen is always, always, the final step in your skin care routine.** Any skin care product applied over a sunscreen dilutes it, lessening its effectiveness, albeit to an unknown degree.

Do you need moisturizer AND sunscreen during the day? Typically, no. That's because the best daytime moisturizers with SPF 30 or greater are formulated with additional skin-beneficial ingredients, so your skin is covered for all aspects of environmental protection, hydration, and anti-aging benefits.

Are sunscreens in a powder, foundation, or spray form as effective as lotion or cream moisturizers? The answer is an unequivocal, yes! When there is an SPF number on any type of sunscreen from a reputable company, it means that the product has been rigorously tested to prove the SPF number is valid. Regardless of the texture or form, if you apply sunscreen correctly, it will deliver the SPF number on the label to your skin.

Where it gets tricky for powder, foundation, and spray sunscreens is in how much you apply. The need to apply sunscreen generously is essential for any SPF product. When it comes to applying powder or foundation sunscreen, if you are not comfortable with applying either type in a visible layer that you can see, you will not be getting adequate sun protection, and not even close to the SPF number on the label. If this describes you, then be sure to liberally apply a moisturizer with sunscreen before you apply any SPF-rated makeup products.

For spray-on sunscreens, the issue is twofold: One is their liquid consistency; the other is the mist the sprayer releases. As you spray this kind of sunscreen on, if you're not careful, the liquid runs and drips right off your body, or you can miss areas if you don't spread it evenly and ensure it's being absorbed. The other issue is the mist—how close you hold the sunscreen spray to your skin. If you hold the nozzle too far from your body, the mist disperses and goes up into the air or falls to the ground, never getting to your skin. We see this all the time at public swimming pools, beaches, or parks where well-meaning parents attempt to apply spray-on sunscreens to squirming kids.

LAYERING SUNSCREEN FOR ADDED PROTECTION

Layering sunscreen (meaning applying one SPF product over another) is a wonderful way to make sure you are applying enough to protect your skin from sun damage. As we've said repeatedly, to truly protect your skin from the ravages of daylight, you must apply sunscreen liberally; it's something most people don't do. However, even if you think you're applying enough sunscreen, layering adds extra insurance. Dozens of studies have shown that anything you can do to get more sunscreen on your skin means you will be better protected!

Layering sunscreens is also very easy. All sunscreen products—regardless of the actives they contain—work together. You can wear a primer with sunscreen, apply a moisturizer with sunscreen, and then follow with a foundation with sunscreen. Just be aware that you shouldn't mix two sunscreens together prior to applying because doing so can affect the formula's ability to protect the skin and, potentially, get an even deposit of the actives. When layering, apply them one after the other, being careful not to "swirl" them together.

It's important for you to understand that when layering sunscreen, for example, applying an SPF 20 over an SPF 30, does not mean you're getting SPF 50 protection. You are getting more protection because you're adding more sunscreen ingredients to your face, which is exactly how a formulator achieves a higher SPF rating, but when you layer different sunscreens, it is not clear what the exact SPF number you end up with is because the combination hasn't been tested. Because of this, you need to make sure one of the SPF products you're applying is rated at least SPF 30 and that you apply it evenly and liberally. Any sunscreen after that is icing on the cake!

DOES SUNSCREEN CAUSE CANCER AND IS IT BAD FOR THE ENVIRONMENT?

This is a difficult discussion because what we know for certain is that sunlight is a carcinogen and is damaging for skin (there is no legitimate scientific debate about that anywhere in the world). We also know that repeated, unprotected exposure to UV light causes skin cancer and premature aging of skin. UV light also triggers other health problems, such as macular degeneration of the eyes (which impairs vision). Being sun-smart includes diligent use of sunscreen plus wearing sunglasses, hats, and sun-protective clothing.

Regarding the environment, there is research into almost all sunscreen ingredients (including mineral sunscreen ingredients) indicating that they can present problems when applied to skin and when they get into our waterways.

An excess of sunscreen ingredients in our oceans has been shown in some studies to destroy coral reefs (think of how many millions of people every year slather their bodies in sunscreen and then go swimming, inadvertently polluting the water). How much of the deteriorating coral reefs and water pollution is attributable to sunscreen, as opposed to the vast amounts of toxic industrial waste and garbage in the world's water supply, is guesswork and inconclusive. However, the concern is understandable.

One sunscreen ingredient that has gotten a lot of negative attention is oxybenzone. For example, in the United States, Hawaii and Florida do not allow the sale of sunscreens that contain oxybenzone because they consider it damaging to coral reefs. As responsible as that may seem, it's a surprisingly futile gesture given that all sunscreen ingredients present issues of environmental safety and have an impact on coral reefs. Why pick on oxybenzone? The environmental concern is well-meaning, but ends up being a misleading focus.

In terms of your health, the research into endocrine disruption or other health problems isn't a straight line to sunscreens. Most of these studies are done on animals and involve using a 100% concentration of the sunscreen ingredient. Even the results of in vivo studies showing that sunscreen ingredients end up in the body do not mean they are doing anything negative. Lots of ingredients end up in the body, from what you eat to what you inhale in the environment, or come into contact with, including plants in skin care products (for example, lavender is an endocrine disruptor). Perhaps those are the health-disrupting culprits and not the sunscreen ingredients. That's what the research doesn't tell.

Ongoing research will reveal more pieces of this puzzle. For now, making any conclusions is getting ahead of what the research shows. In the meantime, what we know for certain is that unprotected sun exposure is bad for your health. We also know conclusively that it causes significant, lasting disruption to every part of your skin, and that sunscreen use plus sun-protective clothing dramatically reduces this daily threat.

In truth, the responsible way to take care of your skin, prevent skin cancer, and take care of the environment is to wear sun-protective clothing (rated UPF 50—UPF stands for Ultraviolet Protection Factor)—both tops and leggings—whether you're at the beach or just out and about during the day. If you will be going into the ocean, sea, lake, or river, UPF clothing is, without question, best for the environment. That's because you will be putting on less sunscreen and, therefore, less sunscreen will be left behind in the water. And, a big bonus is that you will need to reapply far less sunscreen on long days outdoors.

UPF clothing is also the best for your skin. There's another truth about sunscreen most people don't realize: You can never put on enough sunscreen and you should repeatedly reapply it for long days in the sun. This is especially true when swimming if you're wearing a bathing suit that doesn't cover most of your body.

The amount of sunscreen you need to use when wearing a bathing suit is economically prohibitive for most people, especially given the need to frequently reapply if you're swimming or spending a long day outside.

It's also almost impossible to apply it liberally enough all over your body to truly get adequate protection. Plus, that much sunscreen getting into our waterways is irresponsible for our planet. Sun-protective beach clothing and UPF-rated outdoor clothing is sun-smart and budget-brilliant!

To be clear, you still must apply sunscreen liberally to all exposed parts of your body, but, if you cover more of your body with clothing, you'll be using far less sunscreen overall. Better for you and better for the world.

This type of swimwear does a disservice to your skin and marine life:

This is better for your skin and the environment:

THE FACTS ABOUT VITAMIN D AND THE SUN

Just when you thought sun protection couldn't get any more complicated, let us introduce you to vitamin D, an issue that is even more perplexing. Having adequate levels of vitamin D in your circulatory system is imperative for your health because low levels can lead to serious health problems. However, the body can't make vitamin D on its own and there aren't a lot of foods that provide enough vitamin D to the body, which creates a dilemma, because, ironically, the major way the body makes vitamin D is from unprotected sun exposure!

UVB radiation from sunlight triggers skin to make vitamin D. Wearing sunscreen blocks the sun's UVB rays from getting to skin (which is a good thing, because UVB rays cause sunburn), but also can keep the skin from making vitamin D. But, unprotected sun exposure leads to premature aging of skin, and, over time, severely ages skin. Trying to solve one problem (getting enough vitamin D), and causing other problems (skin aging, skin cancer, getting a sunburn), is not a decision anyone should have to make. We know, it's utterly confusing and frustrating.

What is more baffling is when we read recommendations that you should go out in the sun for 15 or 30 minutes every day without sunscreen to get your daily dose of vitamin D. It turns out there is no research showing this recommendation is valid.

How much sun exposure someone needs to make enough vitamin D for their health is unknown because it is based on so many factors. For example, what time of day should you go outside? The intensity of the sun's UVB rays varies with the season, time of day, and geographic location. Is it sufficient to just expose your face and hands or do you need to expose a larger area of skin to get adequate vitamin D? The oft-repeated standard of getting 15 to 30 minutes of unprotected sun exposure every day doesn't make sense, and it certainly isn't practical or good skin care (remember, sun damage begins within the first minute of unprotected skin exposure to daylight).

It's interesting to point out that getting a tan also blocks UVB rays. It's frequently mentioned that Northern Europeans are more vitamin D–deficient than others because of the lack of sun during the winter months in the northern hemisphere. People who wear sunscreen are also said to be more vitamin D–deficient because sunscreen blocks UVB rays, but that hasn't been proven by the research.

Regardless of where you live, it turns out that people with a darker skin color are generally more vitamin D–deficient because the amount of melanin in their skin blocks the sun's UVB rays (melanin is the natural pigment in skin that causes brown skin color and produces a tan) and inhibits vitamin D production.

In real-life scenarios, the concern about sunscreen inhibiting vitamin D is practically a non-issue because most people don't apply sunscreen liberally enough and don't reapply it during long days outdoors. That's why many researchers believe the lack of vitamin D can't be directly correlated to diligent use of sunscreen.

Now that we've completely made your head spin, we're relieved to tell you there is a solution that gets you the vitamin D you need *without* damaging your skin. First, you need to ask your doctor for a blood test to find out if you're vitamin D–deficient. If you are, your doctor can advise you about which vitamin D supplements to take, about how many international units (IU) you should have, and about consuming more vitamin D–enriched foods. This supplement discussion is important because too much vitamin D can cause its own set of problems.

Along with supplements, you can get vitamin D from foods to which it has been added, such as milk, cereals, and orange juice. Good natural sources of vitamin D are fish such as salmon, tuna, sardines, and mackerel as well as beef, shitake mushrooms, and egg yolks.

Just to be clear: There is some research showing that vitamin D supplementation, as opposed to being outside for long periods of time, is not as effective for certain aspects of health. For some disorders (one study looked at Parkinson's disease), vitamin D supplementation increased vitamin D levels, but the increased vitamin D level from supplementation was not associated with the improvement of motor function in comparison to the increased vitamin D level from being outside during the day. However, whether that increased level was the result of sun exposure or of being active was not assessed in the study. Associating vitamin D with the problem is, at best, a stretch.

The most important thing to keep in mind is that unprotected sun exposure is the cause of basal cell and squamous cell skin cancer and, according to the American Cancer Society, "ultraviolet (UV) rays are clearly a major cause of melanoma." There is no question that UV radiation increases your risk of developing some types of skin cancer and that that risk has been increasing every year.

Bottom line: Unprotected sun exposure is the primary cause of skin aging, among many other skin problems. It is also important to realize that tanning blocks the formation of vitamin D. We encourage you to weigh the pros and cons, get your vitamin D levels tested, and ask your physician for guidance.

One more critical point: Indoor tanning salons often claim their machines encourage skin to produce vitamin D, but this is flagrantly NOT true. According to the Skin Cancer Foundation, a tanning bed cannot provide you with the vitamin D you need, nor is it safer than tanning outdoors. Tanning beds emit primarily UVA rays, which generate a tan *and* DNA damage, but UVA is not responsible for vitamin D production. It is the sun's UVB rays (the ones that cause sunburn) that help skin make vitamin D. Tanning beds increase your risk of skin cancer without getting the vitamin D benefit!

WHEN ALL IS SAID AND DONE

Understanding all the details about how to use sunscreen and the often-alarming controversies about sunscreen isn't easy. Still, we strongly believe that research makes it overwhelmingly clear that daily, liberal application of a broad-spectrum SPF 30 sunscreen as the last step in your skin care routine on all exposed parts of your body keeps skin young, healthy, and radiant, and reduces the risk of cancer.

The bottom line: What's best for you and the environment is to wear sun-protective clothing whenever possible, seek shade, avoid basking directly in the sun, and wear sunscreen. AND DON'T FORGET YOUR LIPS! They need sunscreen, too!

PAULA'S CHOICE SKINCARE SUNSCREENS

+ RESIST Super-Light Daily Wrinkle Defense SPF 30 for Normal to Oily Skin
+ RESIST Youth-Extending Hydrating Daily Fluid SPF 50 for Normal to Oily Skin
+ RESIST Skin Restoring Moisturizer SPF 50 for Normal to Dry Skin
+ DEFENSE Essential Glow Moisturizer SPF 30 for All Skin Types
+ SKIN RECOVERY Daily Moisturizing Lotion SPF 30 for Normal to Dry Skin
+ SKIN BALANCING Ultra-Sheer Daily Defense SPF 30 for Normal to Oily Skin
+ CALM Mineral Moisturizer SPF 30 for Normal to Dry Skin
+ CALM Mineral Moisturizer SPF 30 for Normal to Oily Skin
+ CLEAR Ultra-Light Daily Hydrating Fluid SPF 30 for Blemish-Prone Skin
+ Hydralight Shine-Free Mineral Complex SPF 30
+ Moisture Boost Daily Restoring Complex SPF 30
+ Smoothing Primer Serum SPF 30 for All Skin Types
+ Anti-Aging Lip Gloss SPF 40
+ Lipscreen SPF 50
+ On-the-Go Shielding Powder SPF 30

CHAPTER 6

THE BEST ESSENTIAL SKIN CARE ROUTINES

SKIN CARE ROUTINES THAT PROVIDE RESULTS

We promised to help you get the best skin of your life, as this book's title states, and here's the definitive way to achieve it: The only way to have young, healthy skin—and keep it that way for as long as possible—is to start and never stray from using a state-of-the-art skin care routine based on what the scientific research shows works for your skin type and skin concerns! And, it must be a routine you use consistently and change only if your skin concerns change.

With all the information you now have from the previous chapters, the next step is to put together an essential skin care routine. This routine should include a cleanser, exfoliant, daytime moisturizer with sunscreen, and a nighttime moisturizer (the nighttime version doesn't contain sunscreen). You can assemble your own system, but we created several Paula's Choice Skincare routines for different skin types and concerns that can meet all your essential skin care needs. We've done the work for you!

Keep in mind that if you have multiple skin concerns, you may need to add additional products such as treatments, boosters, or serums. We call that an advanced skin care routine. We talk more about advanced routines in the upcoming chapters; for now, the focus is to be sure your essential skin care routine is effective, beneficial, protective, and hydrating, and provides everything else a basic skin care routine should provide. These are the skin care collections Paula's Choice Skincare offers:

+ **RESIST Anti-Aging** has two essential skin care routines, one for normal to dry skin and one for normal to oily skin. These are the quintessential ways to start having younger skin. Our RESIST essential skin care routine for those struggling with normal to oily skin and signs of aging is exceptionally unique. This routine is the first of its kind to address the appearance of wrinkles, skin texture, and uneven skin tone as well as pore size, clogged pores, and breakouts with potent, yet exceptionally lightweight, formulas that leave skin soft and radiant, not greasy or dried out!

+ **SKIN BALANCING** is an essential routine for normal to oily skin that minimizes shine, shrinks the appearance of enlarged pores, creates a brighter and healthier complexion, reduces oily skin, fights multiple signs of aging, and prevents sun damage with lightweight, non-drying formulas that those with oily skin will love.

+ **DEFENSE** for all skin types is our essential skin care routine created to interrupt signs of premature aging, dullness, and discoloration caused by round-the-clock environmental pollutants (including blue light from digital devices) and sun damage. Regular use provides 24-hour environmental protection, reduces the impact of airborne pollutants, protects from sun damage, and nourishes skin. This simple-yet-powerful essential skin care routine is packed with pollution-neutralizing antioxidants, ceramides, and superfoods.

+ **CLEAR for Blemish-Prone Skin** includes two essential skin care routines: One is regular strength for mild acne breakouts; the other is extra strength for moderate to stubborn breakouts. The lightweight formulas are gentle yet tough on breakouts, and work together to provide pore-clearing, redness-reducing, and hydrating benefits. Use it daily to successfully maintain your results. CLEAR also has a unique nighttime moisturizer formulated for acne-prone skin; it protects and hydrates, so you won't need to worry about more breakouts.

+ **CALM** is for extra-sensitive skin, and is even suitable (and truly brilliant) for those with rosacea. This collection has two essential skin care routines, one for normal to dry skin, the other for normal to oily skin. Both offer uniquely formulated products for those struggling with redness-prone, sensitive skin. The assortment of soothing, skin-softening ingredients, which also nourish and restore the skin's barrier, are what makes these formulas so effective. You will see less redness, your skin will look and feel less sensitive, signs of aging will diminish, a smoother skin texture will appear, and you'll also be getting protection from sun damage (a major redness trigger) with an extremely gentle SPF 30 mineral-based sunscreen.

CHAPTER 7

WHEN SKIN NEEDS MORE HELP— ADVANCED ROUTINES

BOOSTERS, SERUMS, AND TREATMENTS

After you start (or if you are already using) a great essential skin care routine, at some point your skin may require more to address specific stubborn concerns. Boosters, serums, and treatments allow you to more precisely target persistent conditions like enlarged pores, clogged pores, markedly uneven skin tone, brown discolorations, advanced sun damage, dehydration, deep wrinkles, loss of firmness, substantial skin barrier damage, and breakouts, among others.

Adding treatment products to your essential skin care routine is what we call an advanced skin care routine. This approach to correcting and restoring skin can be pivotal for getting the best results possible.

WHAT ARE THE DIFFERENCES BETWEEN BOOSTERS, SERUMS, AND TREATMENTS?

Product categories within the cosmetic industry are rarely universal; they vary from company to company. One company's serum may be nothing more than a lotion or moisturizer with some good, hydrating ingredients, while another brand's serums may have state-of-the-art, concentrated formulas to address various skin care needs. That's why, in this section, we describe only what Paula's Choice Skincare's boosters, serums, and treatments are designed to do (which we know very well, because we made them!).

The differences among our boosters, serums, and treatment products might seem subtle, but a closer look reveals interesting nuances that make each one or a combination of a few exceptionally helpful for specific skin types and concerns.

Can a booster, serum, or treatment replace your nighttime moisturizer? Perhaps! Each type of product can work perfectly when worn under a moisturizer; however, for some people, a booster, serum, or treatment product can work fine, either all by itself or layered one over the other, without the separate moisturizer step.

BOOSTERS

Our boosters contain potent concentrations of a single, pivotal ingredient for skin or a blend of a specific ingredient group where the similar structures of each ingredient combine to enhance the results.

Please keep in mind that although our boosters focus on either a single, potent concentration of a superhero ingredient or a blend of related ingredients, they also contain antioxidants, skin-replenishing ingredients, and skin-restoring ingredients. Higher concentrations of a superhero ingredient can bring about amazing outcomes, but even these brilliant ingredients still need support.

Maintaining a long-term relationship with these precious ingredients is how you reap the real benefits. Every day you must help your skin do what it can't do any longer (or do as well) on its own—that's where boosters excel.

PAULA'S CHOICE SKINCARE BOOSTERS

+ **Hyaluronic Acid Booster** increases hydration on multiple levels and visibly plumps skin (all skin types).

+ **Moisture Renewal Oil Booster** hydrates and smooths dry to extremely dry skin.

+ **1% Retinol Booster** fights wrinkles deep within the skin and improves pore function (all skin types).

+ **C15 Super Booster** improves skin discolorations, evens skin tone, and increases skin's natural content of vitamin C to protect from environmental damage (all skin types).

+ **25 Super Booster** contains 25% vitamin C in a silky cream base to combat stubborn problems with skin color and wrinkles, and to ward off environmental damage (all skin types).

+ **10% Niacinamide Booster** meaningfully improves pore size, diminishes breakouts and post-breakout marks, and improves wrinkles, skin barrier, and skin color (all skin types).

+ **Peptide Booster** blends eight targeted peptides known for their ability to instruct skin to function better. It improves skin's firming support system, improves skin discolorations and skin tone, refines texture, and restores pathways that lead to balanced hydration (all skin types).

+ **10% Azelaic Acid Booster** is known for several skin benefits, including reducing breakouts, calming signs of sensitivity, smoothing the appearance of wrinkles, and noticeably improving skin color.

Evolving research leaves no doubt that these targeted ingredients can turn your skin around, solving many problems you may have thought you just had to accept or cover up with makeup.

Each booster is designed to be powerfully effective, yet exceptionally lightweight, and to layer easily with the other products you use. The boosters can be applied alone as a separate step or mixed with serums. They can also be used around the eyes, with or without a separate eye-area product.

SERUMS

Our serums work in harmony with your moisturizer and other skin care products by supplying an advanced, similarly-weighted blend of bio-active antioxidants, skin-replenishing ingredients, and skin-restorative ingredients as additives, much like a vitamin supplement is an additive to your diet. The special characteristics of our serums are balanced concentrations of the critical, supportive ingredients skin needs to be healthy, to further repair itself, and to protect from future damage. It is the concentration of several bio-active ingredients that separate a serum from a moisturizer, as not everything your skin needs can be included in one product.

Our serums also have distinctive *textures* appropriate for different skin types. They range from lightweight, fluid formulas for normal to oily or combination skin to more emollient, silky textures for normal to dry skin.

There's no single "best" serum, so choose yours based on your skin type and concerns. No matter how well-formulated a serum is, if it isn't compatible with your skin type, you'll end up disliking the results, and you won't stick with it.

PAULA'S CHOICE SKINCARE SERUMS

+ **RESIST Super Antioxidant Concentrate Serum** provides extra environmental protection and supercharges normal to dry skin with antioxidants to restore skin health and function.

+ **RESIST Ultra-Light Super Antioxidant Concentrate Serum** provides extra environmental protection and supercharges normal to oily skin with antioxidants to restore skin health and trigger repair, all with a weightless feel.

+ **SKIN BALANCING Super Antioxidant Concentrate Serum** is for those with combination to oily skin, providing extra environmental protection and supercharging the skin with antioxidants and retinol to restore skin health and function.

+ **SKIN RECOVERY Super Antioxidant Concentrate Serum** is for those with normal to dry skin because it contains an ideal assortment of beneficial ingredients to reestablish a dewy, hydrated glow and improve the appearance of wrinkles. Its luxuriously rich, oil-spiked texture absorbs easily.

+ **RESIST Intensive Wrinkle-Repair Retinol Serum** is a moderate-strength retinol product formulated to help repair and prevent visible damage that depletes skin's support structure, which leads to wrinkles.

+ **RESIST Omega+ Complex Serum** delivers powerful soothing and restoring properties for all skin types. It's a great adjunct to a moisturizer when your skin is drier than usual.

+ **EARTH SOURCED Power Berry Serum** contains 15 different fruit extracts, each delivering complementary and synergistic benefits to protect skin from environmental damage, keeping skin healthy, vibrant, and glowing.

+ **CALM Repairing Serum** addresses the needs of those with extra sensitive skin, regardless of skin type. This serum contains high concentrations of potent but gentle ingredients to hydrate, soothe, and strengthen skin's barrier.

+ **DEFENSE Triple Algae Pollution Shield** keeps airborne particulates from sticking to skin, where they would penetrate the pores, causing damage. This weightless, hydrating gel-cream forms an invisible shield to keep skin protected from deeper pollution damage day and night.

TREATMENTS

Our treatment products were developed to address specific concerns with even higher concentrations of some specialty ingredients and to target specific areas of the face or body. These are options when you need a more comprehensive way to add highly specific products to your routine to get the results you want. Every treatment product can also be used with any of our serums or boosters, letting you fully customize your routine.

PAULA'S CHOICE SKINCARE TREATMENTS

+ **CLINICAL 1% Retinol Treatment** is a potent and uniquely formulated retinol solution that hydrates and delivers remarkable anti-aging benefits with a controlled-release delivery system to allow for even, consistent, and soothing absorption.

+ **CLINICAL 20% Niacinamide Treatment** is formulated to address concerns around stubborn enlarged pores, orange peel texture, and the visible effects sun damage has on pores. Its 20% concentration of niacinamide plus supporting ingredients like meadowsweet tighten lax pores, smooth rough texture, and help reduce oil-related bumps.

+ **BHA 9 Treatment** is a one-of-a-kind product with a high concentration of salicylic acid to address extremely clogged pores and stubborn breakouts, and to smooth rough, wrinkled skin. It is for all skin types and can be used nightly where needed as a spot treatment.

+ **Retinol Skin-Smoothing Body Treatment** gently provides the transforming power of retinol and other antioxidants to brighten and give the feeling of soft, firmer skin.

+ **CLEAR Regular Strength Daily Skin Clearing Treatment with 2.5% Benzoyl Peroxide** can be used by anyone at any age who is experiencing mild breakouts. Apply once or twice daily after cleansing and exfoliating.

+ **CLEAR Extra Strength Daily Skin Clearing Treatment with 5% Benzoyl Peroxide** can be used by anyone at any age who is experiencing moderate to stubborn breakouts. Apply once or twice daily after cleansing and exfoliating.

+ **LIP & BODY Treatment Balm** is a rich, concentrated balm formulated to remain on skin and lips overnight. You may never experience dry lips again if you apply it nightly. Lips need care, too, so don't go to bed without it.

HOW TO ADD A BOOSTER, SERUM, OR TREATMENT PRODUCT TO YOUR SKIN CARE ROUTINE

Our boosters, serums, and treatments are versatile, simple to apply, and fast (we want you to get through your skin care routine quickly so you can get on with your day or get to bed). You can layer them in any fashion once or twice per day or use them on alternate days. You can also apply one or more in the morning and a different one at night.

There is really no single right way; everything is adaptable as you develop the method and frequency of application that works best for you. You also don't have to wait for each one to absorb before you apply the next one. Apply one right after the other; none of the formulas interact negatively with the other formulas, nor do they block any of the ingredients from absorbing into skin.

The step-by-step example below shows how you could add one or more of these products to your morning and evening skin care routines. It's simple and fast; no waiting between products. Put one on right after the other and you're done. Just be sure that the last product you apply every morning is sunscreen.

1. Cleanse.
2. Tone.
3. Apply an AHA or BHA exfoliant (can also be used once a day, AM or PM).
4. **Apply one of our boosters, serums, or treatments**, using the lightest, most liquid texture first and finishing with the one that has the thickest texture. If the products have similar textures, layer them based on your personal preference.
5. AM: Apply a skin type–appropriate sunscreen rated SPF 30 or greater.
6. PM: Apply your moisturizer.
7. You can apply an eye-area product twice a day; if your morning eye product does not contain sunscreen, apply it *before* your moisturizer with SPF 30.

CHAPTER 8

ANTI-AGING SKIN CARE

WHY SKIN "AGES," WRINKLES, AND SAGS

Before you spend another dime on products claiming to get rid of wrinkles and firm skin, it's important that you know what causes the signs of aging and how skin care products can either help or make matters worse. Continually hoping that the next product you buy will finally be the answer is a gamble for skin that can waste both your time and money.

All signs of aging are caused by a variety of factors, some that can be handled by skin care products, and others that cannot. Knowing the difference between what skin care products can address and what they can't will get you off the endless merry-go-round of hoping the next product will be the magic bullet you're hoping for. The foremost skin-aging factors are as follows:

Unprotected sun exposure and its cumulative damage. We know we're nagging (okay, … really harassing), but facts are facts, and your daily commitment to applying sunscreen will change how your skin "ages" like no other skin care step. Cumulative unprotected exposure and not being sun-smart is, well, sun-foolish. Sun protection using a product with SPF 30 or greater definitively and instantly reduces both signs of aging and your chances of skin cancer. Using sunscreen 365 days a year will save your skin.

Chronological aging. Every year (every day, really) we get a little older, and each year adds up for your skin, just as it does for your body.

Midlife changes affect the texture, resiliency, and suppleness of skin. The most common sign is that skin becomes less dense and doesn't bounce back when pinched. Enlarged pores can also occur, giving skin an orange-peel texture. You may also experience breakouts for the first time since your teenage years. It is a myth that midlife changes always cause skin to become dry, because often the opposite is what happens.

Facial movements determine what areas begin to show signs of aging first; the parts of your face that you use the most develop fine lines sooner and deeper. That's why facial exercises aren't a good idea and why Botox® injections work so well to (temporarily) eliminate lines caused by muscle movement.

Breakdown of the skin's surface from unprotected sun exposure, environmental assault, or from using skin care products that contain harsh, irritating ingredients.

Pulling or tugging at skin causes it to sag—it's that simple. Whether you're removing makeup or trying to massage products into your skin, if you see your skin move, you are causing it to sag. Pulling skin up, down, or sideways stretches the elastin fibers in skin and doing this repeatedly stretches them to their breaking point. You need to preserve the elastin fibers you have because they are responsible for skin's resilience and ability to bounce back into place. It's also especially important because, unlike collagen, it's very difficult to get skin to make more elastin.

Your overall health and disease. We have control, to some degree, over how healthy we are in terms of lifestyle choices (no smoking, a healthy diet, limiting alcohol intake, exercise), but certain diseases are beyond our control and can take a toll on how our skin looks.

All of these factors decrease the youthful, healthy, protective, and reparative substances in skin. This includes its natural supply of antioxidants, skin-replenishing ingredients, and skin-restoring ingredients. Reduced levels of each leaves skin more vulnerable to the effects of internal and external aging.

Armed with this information, you have a better handle on the improvements you can realistically expect to see from even the best skin care products. You'll also be able to more easily spot cosmetics claims that are beyond the capability of even the best skin care products.

CAN ANTI-AGING PRODUCTS HELP?

The answer is unequivocally: Yes! Anti-aging products can make all the difference in the world because skin aging is not as much about getting older as it is about sun damage and how you take care of your skin. Consistently using the best products for your skin type and skin concerns can provide astounding results.

The essence of a great anti-aging skin care routine is to stop ongoing sun damage and give skin the substances it can no longer produce for itself because of that damage. The goal is to help restore skin's normal function, structure, and skin tone as much as possible. It is also vital to protect skin from further damage by repairing its barrier and restoring the healthy substances that young skin has in abundance.

Remember, achieving such results is never about what any one product or ingredient (no matter how much it's hyped) can do. Just like a healthy diet isn't about eating only one food or one nutrient; skin is far more complicated than any one ingredient or any one product can address.

We've been stressing throughout this book mandatory ingredients and products that you need to fight skin aging. As a reminder, here are the ingredients and the product types you should be using:

Topically applied antioxidants, without question, are essential for getting and keeping younger-looking skin. The more antioxidants included in your skin care products, the better they're able to interrupt external influences on skin before deeper damage occurs.

Young, healthy skin naturally contains a wealth of **skin-replenishing substances** that keep it smooth, retain moisture, help skin resist environmental assault, stay supple and resilient, and lessen the chances of redness and sensitivity. Age and unprotected sun exposure decrease skin's ability to make these skin-natural substances and deplete the little it can still make on its own.

Skin-restoring ingredients are fascinating; they literally work to help skin reorganize, rebalance, rejuvenate, and reestablish itself. It's an exciting and intriguing area of skin care—these are ingredients your skin care products must contain!

Gentle leave-on AHA (glycolic or lactic acid) or BHA (salicylic acid) exfoliants. When these types of non-abrasive exfoliating products are well-formulated, they gently exfoliate the surface of skin, just as skin did naturally when we were young. They provide a nearly instant smoother, softer, more radiant, even-toned, resilient, and less wrinkled appearance by revealing the younger skin hiding beneath:

+ BHA and AHAs help create smoother and firmer-looking skin.
+ BHA and AHAs greatly diminish dry, flaky, rough, uneven skin.
+ BHA noticeably minimizes the size of enlarged pores.
+ BHA diminishes clogged pores, white bumps, and other types of breakouts. (Some people with clogged pores and bumps have success with AHAs, but the research overwhelmingly supports BHA for these concerns.)

Moisturizers loaded with all the beneficial ingredients we've been talking about, which are antioxidants, skin-replenishing, and skin-restoring ingredients.

Boosters, serums, or treatment products that help address your specific skin concerns. These exceptional ingredients must be present at higher strengths or concentrations, in pure forms, or in special delivery systems to have the most positive impact on skin. Because of these formulary considerations and skin care needs for advanced stubborn concerns, one product can't include everything you need in the right concentrations to achieve the results you want.

Sunscreen! You already know the primary reasons why sunscreen is critically important for skin, but you can also do your own "test" to see how unprotected sun exposure is aging your skin. Compare skin on the parts of your body that have been protected from the sun (those areas not routinely exposed to daylight) with skin on the parts that have been exposed to sun. The more protected parts of skin are rarely, if ever, wrinkled, discolored, or crepey, and don't sag very much (at least not as fast as the areas exposed to the sun). Just compare skin on the underside of your forearm, abdomen, or backside to skin on your hands, chest, or face. Areas with little to no sun damage look younger and "newer" because they haven't been subject to the cumulative aging and wrinkling effects of unprotected sun exposure.

WHEN SHOULD YOU BEGIN USING ANTI-AGING PRODUCTS?

The answer: You're never too young to start using anti-aging products. You just need to think differently about what fighting premature aging or aging skin means. Another way to look at it is the same way you look at your diet. Regardless of your age, eating a healthy diet helps keep your body healthier and acting younger, longer—the same is true for skin. Giving skin the ingredients it's hungry for and being sun-smart is the overarching lifetime skin care strategy everyone should follow.

Being sun-smart is even more true now that we know about the exposome factors (inflammatory factors) discussed in Chapter 2. What you do throughout your life to reduce inflammation is important every day of your life, from birth onward.

With that in mind, just as it doesn't make sense to wait until you are unhealthy or "older" to start a healthy diet or lifestyle, the same is true for an anti-aging skin care routine. If anything, the opposite is true: The sooner you start using anti-aging products, the more likely your skin will reflect that effort by slowing the signs of aging, with exponentially beautiful results.

Even as a child, it's important to use products with skin-healthy ingredients (antioxidants and skin-replenishing ingredients are beneficial for children, too). For example, when you're going to bathe your baby, the type of cleanser you choose should be really gentle because it will also affect skin's barrier. Sunscreen is a requirement (pediatricians around the world recommend sunscreen on the areas of a baby's skin that are exposed to the sun), and avoiding products with irritating ingredients is also exceptionally important.

A child's skin is extremely vulnerable to everything it comes in contact with because its barrier function is still developing, which means you should never apply skin-sensitizing ingredients (particularly essential oils, which products for babies often contain) to your baby's skin.

Beginning to use products loaded with impressive skin-protective ingredients before you start seeing signs of aging will put you on track for having and keeping the skin you want now and in the future.

RECOMMENDED ANTI-AGING PRODUCTS FROM PAULA'S CHOICE SKINCARE FOR NORMAL TO DRY SKIN

Cleanser
+ **RESIST Optimal Results Hydrating Cleanser**

Toner
+ **RESIST Advanced Replenishing Toner**

AHA Exfoliants
+ **RESIST Daily Smoothing Treatment with 5% AHA**
+ **RESIST Advanced Smoothing Treatment with 10% AHA**

Serum
+ **RESIST Super Antioxidant Concentrate Serum**
+ **RESIST Intensive Wrinkle-Repair Retinol Serum** (all skin types)

Booster
+ **Moisture Renewal Oil Booster**
+ **10% Azelaic Acid Booster**
+ **Hyaluronic Acid Booster**
+ **Peptide Booster** (all skin types)

Treatment
+ **CLINICAL 1% Retinol Treatment** (all skin types)
+ **CLINICAL Triple Action Dark Spot Eraser 7% AHA and 2% Hydroquinone Lotion**
  (all skin types)

Eye Cream
+ **RESIST Anti-Aging Eye Cream**
+ **CLINICAL Ceramide-Enriched Firming Eye Cream**

Mask
+ **Rehydrating Moisture Mask**
+ **Radiance Renewal Mask** (all skin types)

Daytime Moisturizer with SPF
+ **RESIST Skin Restoring Moisturizer with SPF 50**

Nighttime Moisturizers
+ **RESIST Barrier Repair Moisturizer with Retinol**
+ **RESIST Intensive Repair Cream with Retinol**

RECOMMENDED ANTI-AGING PRODUCTS FROM PAULA'S CHOICE SKINCARE FOR NORMAL TO OILY SKIN

Cleanser

+ **RESIST Perfectly Balanced Foaming Cleanser**

Toner

+ **RESIST Weightless Advanced Repairing Toner**

BHA Exfoliants

+ **RESIST Daily Pore-Refining Treatment 2% BHA**
+ **RESIST Advanced Pore-Refining Treatment 4% BHA**

Serum

+ **RESIST Ultra-Light Super Antioxidant Concentrate Serum**
+ **Omega + Complex Serum** (all skin types)

Booster

+ **1% Retinol Booster** (all skin types)
+ **10% Niacinamide Booster** (all skin types)
+ **Hyaluronic Acid Booster** (all skin types)
+ **Peptide Booster** (all skin types)

Treatment

+ **CLINICAL 20% Niacinamide Treatment**
+ **CLINICAL Triple Action Dark Spot Eraser Gel 2% BHA and 2% Hydroquinone Gel** (all skin types)

Eye Cream

+ **RESIST Anti-Aging Eye Cream**
+ **CLINICAL Ceramide-Enriched Firming Eye Cream**

Mask

+ **Pore Clarifying Charcoal Gel Mask**

Daytime Moisturizer with SPF

+ **RESIST Youth-Extending Daily Hydrating Fluid SPF 50**
+ **RESIST Super Light Daily Wrinkle Defense SPF 30**

Nighttime Moisturizer

+ **RESIST Anti-Aging Clear Skin Hydrator**

CHAPTER 9

MANAGING OILY SKIN

WHAT CAUSES OILY SKIN

When your skin produces a balanced amount of oil (meaning not too much and not too little), it does wonderful things: maintains hydration, smoothness, and softness; helps skin maintain a healthy microbiome; and protects skin from environmental assault. When too much oil is produced in the pore, it is delivered to skin in what many people describe as feeling and looking like an oil spill. Trying to manage oily skin is not easy; in fact, it's one of the more difficult skin types to normalize.

Oily skin is almost always the result of genetically predetermined hormonal changes in the body that typically occur during the teenage years; however, these hormonal changes, especially for women (as many of us know all too well), can occur at any age. You can't get hormones under control with skin care products, which is a big reason that oily skin is so difficult to manage.

Making matters worse, an unwanted side effect of oily skin is that you often end up also struggling with clogged, enlarged pores, breakouts, and roughness.

Not sure if you have oily skin? It's recognizable by a few classic characteristics:

+ Your face is shiny only an hour or two after cleansing and appears greasy by midday.
+ Your makeup seems to "slide" off or disappear in a few hours after you apply it.
+ The shiniest parts of your face have clogged pores and tend to break out. Your skin can be oily mostly on your nose, chin, and forehead (where the face has the most oil glands), but it can also be oily everywhere else.

GETTING SHINE UNDER CONTROL—THE DON'T LIST

The first step in caring for oily skin is to take a critical look at your current skin care routine because there are products you might be using that are making matters worse and there are probably products you should be using to reduce the oil flow. Take these recommendations to heart, as they will be game changers for your skin.

Don't irritate skin. Research makes it clear that irritating your skin makes everything worse, especially for oily skin. Soap and bar cleansers are not your friends because they can be drying, which is the exact opposite of being gentle to your skin, and dry skin won't stop oil production. Moreover, the typical ingredients that keep bar soaps and cleansers in their bar form leave a film on skin that can clog pores.

Avoid harsh scrubs and cleansing brushes with stiff bristles, as both can cause micro-tears in skin, disrupting and harming skin's surface. This disruption, in turn, makes acne worse and prevents post-acne marks from healing.

Research has shown that irritating oily skin triggers it to produce more oil. It seems that the hormones that cause acne can be stimulated by surface inflammation that gradually moves down the pore lining, triggering more oil production. Stopping irritation can make every aspect of your skin better, but it can also decrease oil production to some degree.

Avoid products that make your skin tingle (such as those that contain menthol, mint, eucalyptus, and lemon) or that contain SD or denatured alcohol listed among the first few ingredients. These may feel like they are de-greasing your oily skin or doing something good because of the tingling sensation, but they're actually making matters worse. A tingling sensation means skin is being irritated, which can trigger the oil glands to produce more oil (research about this from years ago was shocking at first, and rocked the world of skin care for those of us with oily, acne-prone skin). This is a very important fact to keep in mind because lots of products claiming to be good for oily skin and clogged pores often contain problematic, harsh ingredients.

Avoid products that are thick or too emollient as these will only make oily skin feel more oily because of their texture. They're great for dry skin, but they aren't what someone with oily skin needs. Steer clear of products that have a thick, heavy, or solid texture, such as solid stick-styled foundations, thick concealers, or rich, emollient moisturizers, lotions, facial oils, or balms. All such thick products are likely to make skin feel more oily and potentially clog pores. Instead, use only liquid, thin, lightweight serums, gels, or weightless lotion moisturizers or boosters for both skin care and makeup.

GETTING SHINE UNDER CONTROL—THE DO LIST

The following essential skin care routine will help get your oily skin to slow down, at least to some extent, and will absolutely help protect it from premature aging and environmental damage. This routine will also keep it hydrated and smooth without making the skin feel greasy or clogging pores.

Cleanse twice daily with a gentle, water-soluble cleanser. Ideally, a cleanser should rinse without leaving a hint of residue or a tight, dry feeling. It should also be fragrance-free because fragrance, whether from essential oils, plant extracts, or synthetic sources, irritates skin. Essential oils are always a negative for oily skin because of the irritation they cause.

Gently exfoliate with a completely non-abrasive leave-on BHA gel or liquid. Oily skin tends to have an extra buildup of dead skin on the surface and a thickened pore lining. Exfoliating skin's surface and inside the pore lining is the best way to remove that buildup, shrink and unclog pores, and control breakouts, all while making skin feel unbelievably smoother. A unique benefit of BHA is that it can also calm skin, which is very helpful for reducing oil production in the pore and diminishing breakouts.

Apply sun protection 365 days a year, rain or shine. Even if you have oily skin, a sunscreen is essential for reducing the risk of early signs of aging and skin cancer, helping skin heal post-breakout marks, and just about anything else you want to improve with your skin. If you've avoided sunscreens because the ones you've tried are too greasy or occlusive, or if you were afraid they'd clog pores, we present at the end of this chapter recommendations that hopefully will change your impression of sunscreens for good. If you wear foundation, you can also use one that contains sunscreen.

Apply a moisturizer at night, but don't use a traditional one. Just because you have oily skin doesn't mean you should forgo giving your skin the highest quality ingredients to keep it healthy, hydrated, renewed, and refreshed with less redness. To give your skin these wonderful nourishing ingredients without adding emollients that feel greasy and clog pores, use only extremely lightweight liquids, gels, or weightless serum formulations. You'll get the remarkable benefits of these ingredients without any of the "weight" traditional moisturizing creams and lotions impart.

Use an oil-absorbing product during the day. Even with all our research-backed recommendations, when you have oily skin, there are simply limitations to what skin care products can do. That means you'll probably still need to use an oil-absorbing product during the day. The best oil-absorbing products contain ingredients such as clay (and it doesn't have to be a special clay, despite the claims made about miracle versions from volcanoes or rare earths), mineral powders, and starches that work to varying degrees to keep oily skin fresh and matte.

RECOMMENDED PRODUCTS FROM PAULA'S CHOICE SKINCARE FOR OILY SKIN

Cleanser
+ **SKIN BALANCING Oil-Reducing Cleanser**
+ **CALM Nourishing Cleanser for Normal to Oily Skin**

Toner
+ **SKIN BALANCING Pore-Reducing Toner**
+ **CALM Soothing Toner Normal to Oily Skin**

BHA Exfoliant
+ **SKIN PERFECTING 2% BHA Liquid Exfoliant** (all skin types)
+ **SKIN PERFECTING 2% BHA Gel Exfoliant** (all skin types)
+ **CALM 1% BHA Lotion Exfoliant** (all skin types)

Serum
+ **SKIN BALANCING Super Antioxidant Concentrate Serum**
+ **CALM Repairing Serum** (all skin types)
+ **DEFENSE Triple Algae Pollution Shield** (all skin types)

Booster
+ **1% Retinol Booster** (all skin types)
+ **10% Niacinamide Booster** (all skin types)

Eye Cream
+ **RESIST Anti-Aging Eye Gel**

Oil-Absorbing
+ **SHINE STOPPER Instant Matte Finish**

Mask
+ **Pore-Clarifying Charcoal Gel Mask**
+ **SKIN BALANCING Oil-Absorbing Mask**

Daytime Moisturizers with SPF
+ **SKIN BALANCING Ultra-Sheer Daily Defense SPF 30**
+ **CALM Mineral Moisturizer SPF 30 Normal to Oily Skin**

Nighttime Moisturizer
+ **SKIN BALANCING Invisible Finish Moisture Gel**
+ **CALM Restoring Moisturizer Normal to Oily Skin**

CHAPTER 10

KEEPING DRY SKIN HYDRATED

WHAT CAUSES DRY SKIN

When skin's surface is healthy and intact, its water content is somewhere between 10% and 30%. If the surface is not healthy and intact, or if the underlying water system (aquaporins) is damaged, skin can't stay hydrated as it should. The result: skin loses water, leading to dry, dehydrated skin.

It turns out that keeping skin's water content balanced is not actually about adding more "water" to skin; in fact, too much water is not a good thing! Too much "water/moisture" from soaking in a bathtub or taking a long shower is a problem for skin because excess water disrupts skin's surface, making it difficult to keep its water content normal—the result is dry, flaky, dehydrated, and crepey skin.

Skin becomes dry for many of the reasons we've been discussing throughout this book. Skin loses its ability to maintain normal moisture levels from the surface to the lower layers. Health, what you inherit from your parents, and age are significant factors, but what certainly makes it worse is unprotected sun exposure. Over time, sun exposure destroys the surface and the lower layers of skin so it can't function normally. Adding to the severity of that problem, or often even causing it, is using skin care products that contain harsh, drying, irritating ingredients (many people with dry skin think they can scrub signs of dryness away, but scrubbing almost always makes matters worse).

In terms of unprotected sun exposure, just like we discussed in the Chapter 8 on anti-aging skin care, if you're over 30, compare skin on the parts of your body that are routinely exposed to daylight with skin on the parts of your body that are rarely exposed. You'll probably notice that the sun-protected areas are not dry or are barely dry; just look at the underside of your forearm or your backside. That's because those areas with little to no sun damage don't suffer from the range of problems caused by the cumulative damage of unprotected daily exposure to UV light.

WHAT NOT TO DO FOR DRY SKIN

Anything you do that inhibits your skin's ability to keep water safely where it belongs either causes dry skin or makes dry skin worse. As always, the first step to improving dry skin is to stop doing things that make it worse, which include the following:

+ Don't use bar soaps or bar cleansers of any kind as these are always more drying than a gentle, skin-smoothing water-soluble cleanser. This is true from the neck down, too.
+ Make sure your water-soluble cleansers have the right formula. Don't use any that leave skin feeling tight and dry.
+ Avoid at all costs products with ingredients that are drying or sensitizing, or that cause redness, such as essential oils, denatured or SD alcohol, peppermint, menthol, mint, citrus, eucalyptus, and fragrance (whether from essential oils, fragrant plant extracts, or synthetic sources). They also cause progressive barrier damage and water loss.
+ Avoid excessive exposure to hot water or steam. Both dehydrate skin and can trigger or worsen redness, broken capillaries, and ashy discolorations.
+ Never use abrasive scrubs or cleansing brushes that tear at skin's surface. This disrupts skin's ability to hold onto water, a significant problem for all skin types, but especially for dry skin.
+ Never allow your skin to be exposed to the sun without sun protection. (Sorry, we had to say it yet again, we can't help ourselves.)
+ Don't smoke and avoid secondhand smoke. Exposing skin to cigarette smoke literally kills skin and hurts its overall health.

All of the above disrupt skin's surface, which, in turn, leads to water loss and destroys the vital substances in skin that allow it to hold onto just the right amount of moisture. The next step is what you need to do now to keep your skin hydrated and moist.

HOW TO CARE FOR DRY SKIN

Regardless of the root cause of your dry skin, the fundamental need is to help skin achieve and maintain a healthy moisture balance; that is, to put disrupted skin back together as best you can. When skin lacks the natural substances it needs to remain intact, the job of great skin care products is to generously and abundantly replenish those substances. Here's how you can do that:

Wear sunscreen rated SPF 30+ daily, rain or shine, hot or cold weather. Unprotected exposure to the sun slowly but surely impairs skin's ability to hold on to moisture and to feel smooth and soft.

Cleanse your face with a gentle, non-irritating, water-soluble cleanser that leaves your skin soft and soothed, with no tight or dry feeling whatsoever.

Use moisturizers, serums, boosters, and treatment products that are filled to the brim with antioxidants, skin-restoring ingredients, and skin-replenishing ingredients that help skin keep a healthy, normal balance of water in all layers and prevent water loss.

Use a non-abrasive, gentle leave-on AHA or BHA exfoliant. Shedding the buildup of dead surface skin is something your skin did efficiently all by itself when it was young and not yet damaged from unprotected sun exposure. When skin can no longer exfoliate efficiently on its own, it becomes dull, rough, dry, and dehydrated. In that condition, it doesn't absorb skin care products very well either, thus limiting their potential for making a difference. Using a gentle leave-on AHA or BHA exfoliant as part of your skin care routine, whether essential or advanced, will help skin shed in a more natural, youthful manner to reveal the plump, younger-looking skin hiding below. Another amazing benefit of AHAs and BHA is that they also increase hydration, often overnight!

For very dry skin, using a blend of pure non-fragrant, nourishing plant oils, such as almond, argan, borage, coconut, evening primrose, jojoba seed, olive, or safflower oils, can make a significant difference. Apply them after cleansing, toning, and exfoliating, but before applying your moisturizer.

Don't forget your lips. Lips are the least capable of staying smooth and soft, so don't leave them naked, day or night. During the day, apply and reapply an emollient lipstick or gloss that provides sun protection (an incredibly important anti-aging moisturizing step for your lips). At night, don't go to sleep without protecting your lips with an emollient lip balm, which must be completely non-irritating and must not contain fragrance of any kind (e.g., essential oils, fragrant plant extracts, or synthetic sources), menthol, or camphor because they'll only make dry lips worse.

DOES DRINKING MORE WATER HELP?

This is one of those beauty myths that refuses to go away—here are the facts: Although drinking eight glasses of water a day is a good idea for your body, you can't rely on it to get rid of dry skin. If that's all it took, very few people would have dry skin. The causes of and solutions for dry skin are far more complex than just drinking water.

Prior to 2016, there was no research showing that drinking a lot of water would have any impact on skin. A study published in *Clinical Cosmetic Investigative Dermatology* (August 2016, pages 413–415) showed that drinking more water *did* have a positive impact on skin; however, the study concluded that it would take just less than a *gallon* of water (8 [8 oz.] glasses = half a gallon, 16 [8 oz.] glasses = a gallon) to gain a statistical improvement in your skin. But, a "statistical" improvement does not mean that you would see or feel a change; it merely reflects what the technical data measured.

Although it was a complex study, and had only 49 participants, it was an interesting analysis of the effect of water consumption on skin. On the basis of this one study, you shouldn't start downing a gallon of water in hopes to skin improve your skin, and a "statistical" improvement does not mean that you won't still experience dry skin.

Whatever quantity of water you decide to drink, drinking water will not replace the skin care recommendations we strongly urge you to follow. Getting the best skin of your life involves not only what you eat and drink, but also what you apply to skin's surface to keep it healthy looking and hydrated.

RECOMMENDED PRODUCTS FROM PAULA'S CHOICE SKINCARE FOR DRY SKIN

Cleanser
+ **SKIN RECOVERY Softening Cream Cleanser**
+ **CALM Nourishing Cleanser Normal to Dry Skin**

Toner
+ **SKIN RECOVERY Enriched Calming Toner**
+ **CALM Soothing Toner Normal to Dry Skin**

AHA Exfoliant
+ **SKIN PERFECTING 8% AHA Lotion**

BHA Exfoliant
+ **CALM 1% BHA Lotion Exfoliant** (all skin types)

Serum
+ **SKIN RECOVERY Super Antioxidant Concentrate Serum**
+ **CALM Repairing Serum** (all skin types)
+ **Omega + Complex Serum** (all skin types)

Booster
+ **10% Azelaic Acid Booster** (all skin types)
+ **Moisture Renewal Oil Booster**
+ **Hyaluronic Acid Booster** (all skin types)
+ **Peptide Booster** (all skin types)

Mask
+ **SKIN RECOVERY Hydrating Treatment Mask**
+ **Rehydrating Moisture Mask**

Daytime Moisturizers with SPF

+ SKIN RECOVERY Daily Moisturizing Lotion SPF 30
+ CALM Mineral Moisturizer SPF 30 Normal to Dry Skin

Nighttime Moisturizer

+ SKIN RECOVERY Replenishing Moisturizer
+ CLINICAL Ultra-Rich Moisturizer
+ CALM Restoring Moisturizer Normal to Dry Skin

Eye Cream

+ CLINICAL Ceramide-Enriched Firming Eye Cream
+ RESIST Anti-Aging Eye Cream

CHAPTER 11

BALANCING COMBINATION SKIN

WHAT IS COMBINATION SKIN?

Combination skin is exactly what it sounds like—having two skin types at the same time—but it usually means having oily skin and dry skin. Most people with combination skin have oily skin around the nose, center of the forehead, and top of the cheek bone, with drier areas everywhere else. For others, however, combination skin might be when the skin all over the face feels tight and dry, but there is also a layer of oil sitting on top of it.

Regardless of the type of combination skin you have, what you do to lessen those problems is the same. Thankfully, this is one skin condition that can be relatively easy to get under control.

WHAT CAUSES COMBINATION SKIN?

A variety of factors contribute to combination skin. Sometimes it's just genetics, meaning you inherited the trait, with some areas of your face feeling dry and others feeling oily, but that's not typical. Far more often, skin that is oily and dry at the same time is the result of the skin care products being used. The wrong skin care products can cause some areas of your face to be more oily than they would be normally and other areas to be drier than they would be normally.

You probably already know what we're going to tell you, but here it is again: Using products that contain harsh, abrasive, or irritating ingredients will inevitably dehydrate, damage, and dry out some areas of your face and will stimulate more oil production in the parts that are already oil-prone.

When your skin is naturally oily, and you use products that you think will dry up the oil or you scrub away at clogged pores, you're making skin worse. If you like products that make your skin tingle because you think that means they are working, it adds up to trouble. These drying, irritating products make the surface of skin dry and flaky, but they don't stop your skin from producing excess oil (if anything, research shows that they stimulate more oil production), so you will also get a noticeable layer of oil on top of the dry, dehydrated layer.

WHICH PRODUCTS TO USE FOR COMBINATION SKIN

The major thing to keep in mind when you have combination skin is that all the products you use must be gentle, loaded with beneficial, protective, and skin-restoring ingredients, and provide hydration that isn't heavy or greasy. You also can use oil-absorbing products where needed, but avoid using these on the dry areas.

Once you begin using the right products, you'll be able to determine if your skin is truly combination, or if the problem was created by the products you were using. With this answer revealed, the next step is to decide which products to use all over your face and which products to apply only to one area or another. For the dry areas, you may need to use more emollient products; for the oily areas, you may need to apply products that are more fluid/liquid, or that have a gel or very thin lotion texture.

The following guidelines may help get you on the right path with options that gently balance skin.

Use a gentle, soothing, gel-based or foaming cleanser. Regardless of the texture, a cleanser must be gentle and leave skin soft without feeling tight or dry.

Use a gentle, non-abrasive, leave-on beta hydroxy acid (BHA, salicylic acid) exfoliant. This is an optimal choice for exfoliating combination skin and significantly improving, sometimes overnight, both your dry skin *and* your oily skin.

A BHA exfoliant helps skin invisibly shed the built-up layers of dead skin that it can't take care of on its own. BHA unclogs pores, lessens oily skin because it reduces inflammation, and at the same time gently smooths away rough, dry skin so it feels far less flaky or tight. For combination skin, a gel, weightless fluid, or serum-textured BHA exfoliant is best.

Sun protection is mandatory even on the oily areas of your face. Daily use prevents premature aging of the skin, helps skin repair itself, and keeps the surface of skin healthy and resilient. Choose a lightweight sunscreen with SPF 30 or greater, ideally with a soft matte finish. Over the dry areas, you may need to prep skin with a light serum or fluid-texture booster first and then apply your matte-finish sunscreen over it.

Use a nighttime moisturizer with a gel, serum, fluid, or even liquid texture that contains all the amazing ingredients we hope you now know by heart: antioxidants, skin-replenishing ingredients, and skin-restoring ingredients. These ingredients are imperative if you want to help calm skin, lessen oil production, and improve dry areas. If you have very dry areas, you may need to apply a richer, more emollient moisturizer just to those areas, being sure to blend away from the oil-prone areas.

Putting together a skin care routine for combination skin is a bit more tricky than it is for other skin types because it often means you must apply products with different textures to different areas or layer products in some areas. Once you start using the right products, however, your skin will start feeling and looking better rather quickly.

RECOMMENDED PRODUCTS FROM PAULA'S CHOICE SKINCARE FOR COMBINATION SKIN

Cleanser
+ **SKIN BALANCING Oil-Reducing Cleanser**
+ **DEFENSE Hydrating Gel-to-Cream Cleanser** (all skin types)

Toner
+ **SKIN BALANCING Pore-Reducing Toner**
+ **CALM Soothing Toner Normal to Oily Skin**

BHA Exfoliant
+ **SKIN PERFECTING 2% BHA Liquid Exfoliant** (all skin types)
+ **SKIN PERFECTING 2% BHA Gel Exfoliant** (all skin types)

Serum
+ **SKIN BALANCING Super Antioxidant Concentrate Serum with Retinol**
+ **DEFENSE Antioxidant Pore Purifier** (all skin types)
+ **DEFENSE Triple Algae Pollution Shield** (all skin types)

Booster
+ **Hyaluronic Acid Booster** (all skin types)
+ **10% Niacinamide Booster** (all skin types)
+ **1% Retinol Booster** (all skin types)
+ **Moisture Renewal Oil Booster** (to be used only over dry areas)

Mask
+ **RADIANCE Renewal Mask** (to be used over dry areas)
+ **Pore Clarifying Charcoal Gel Mask** (to be used over oily areas)
+ **CLEAR Purifying Mask** (for blemish-prone skin)

Eye Cream or Eye Gel

+ **RESIST Anti-Aging Eye Cream**
+ **RESIST Anti-Aging Eye Gel**
+ **CLINICAL Ceramide-Enriched Firming Eye Cream**
+ **Omega + Complex Eye Cream**

Daytime Moisturizer with SPF

+ **DEFENSE Essential Glow Moisturizer SPF 30** (all skin types)
+ **SKIN BALANCING Ultra-Sheer Daily Defense SPF 30**

Nighttime Moisturizer

+ **Probiotic Nutrient Moisturizer** (all skin types)
+ **CBD Skin Transformative Treatment Milk** (all skin types)
+ **DEFENSE Nightly Reconditioning Moisturizer** (all skin types)
+ **SKIN BALANCING Invisible Finish Moisture Gel**

CHAPTER 12

TREATING ACNE AT ANY AGE

UNDERSTANDING ACNE

Acne is one of the most troublesome and common skin care problems for people around the world, and one of the most emotionally frustrating. Although acne is most often associated with teenagers and the onset of puberty, you can suffer from it at any age. Even if you never had acne when you were young, it can still occur in your 20s, 30s, 40s, 50s, and even linger on through your 60s.

Most of us are familiar with acne to some degree—even if we don't know the specifics, we all know what it looks like. Acne's textbook definition describes it as an inflammatory skin disorder that occurs when hormones (mostly androgens) fluctuate. Consequently, acne is far more typical for teenagers because puberty causes a hormonal frenzy in the body.

Once adulthood is reached, men's hormones stabilize, while women's can continue to be erratic, especially around their periods or when midlife menopausal changes start happening (which explains the tendency for women to break out just before their periods and throughout their lives). This is why acne is more common in adult women than in adult men.

Acne results primarily from a hormone imbalance that causes the oil glands (in the pores) to produce too much oil. When the pore can't release all the oil being produced, it begins to clog. The clog quickly gets mixed with more oil and dead skin, causing a thick, waxy accumulation, making the clogged pore worse. This mixture of dead skin and oil allows bacteria to flourish, resulting in inflammation. The inflammation and bacteria cause pus, culminating in the eruption of a red bump with a white fluid-filled sac in the middle. In short, you have a pimple (a word we just hate).

What we want to impress on you, first and foremost, is that you do not want to make those red blemishes any redder! So, even though you might want to try to scrub away acne or use drying, tingling products hoping to reduce oil production, that will only make matters worse. Instead, acne-prone skin needs gentle, soothing products that do not increase redness, irritation, or dryness.

You must only use anti-acne products that diminish acne without damaging skin—these types of products do exist! There are gentle products that contain the active ingredients proven to get acne under control and not make it worse. Please don't ignore what the research says—acne-prone skin must be handled gently to get it under control.

ADULT ACNE VERSUS TEENAGE ACNE

It's a fundamental fact that regardless of your age, gender, nationality, where you live, skin color, or race, the best way to treat acne is the same for everyone.

The types of products to choose and the active ingredients they must contain (and what they should not contain) are universal. In short, no matter who you are, stop doing the things that make acne worse and start using products and practices that make it better.

There may be a difference in the products that teens use and that adults use because the adults need additional products to address signs of aging, skin discolorations, and other effects of sun damage. Those additional products can be easily included in an anti-acne skin care routine because there are some whose formulas won't make acne worse and that still address signs of aging. Another plus: The skin-restoring properties of the best anti-aging products will help skin recover from acne breakouts faster than they might otherwise. The products recommended at the end of this chapter are a suggested skin care routine to fight both acne and aging.

THE BASICS FOR EVERYONE

Keep skin clean, but don't overdo it. Thorough cleansing is a good thing because it removes excess oil, debris, impurities, and makeup, all of which contribute to clogged pores and create the conditions that acne needs to occur. But, over-cleansing, being too rough, cleansing too often, or using harsh cleansers, scrubs, or cleansing brushes with stiff bristles aggravate skin and make it redder than it already is—that is not a good thing!

GENTLE cleansing is an absolute must. The best way is to cleanse your face twice daily with an effective, but skin-softening, water-soluble cleanser. You can use a double cleansing method if you need to remove makeup, which involves cleansing your face twice with one cleanser or using two different cleansers, rinsing between uses.

You must steer clear of all bar soaps and bar cleansers—they can be drying and irritating and can leave a film or residue on your skin (just like they do on your soap dish), which, in turn, can clog pores and limit the effectiveness of any anti-acne products you apply after cleansing.

Avoid all skin care and makeup products that contain harsh or irritating ingredients (even a little bit of irritation is bad for skin). Acne is red, and anything you do to make your skin more red adds fuel to the fire, worsening all types of acne. Using irritating products increases redness and damages the surface of skin, inhibiting the healing process. *Plus,* research shows that anything that irritates your skin can directly stimulate oil production in the oil gland due to the presence of nerve endings that trigger the production of acne-causing hormones! Obviously, this makes acne worse. Unfortunately, many skin care and makeup products, including many claiming to be for acne-prone skin, contain problematic, drying ingredients.

To reduce acne and the accompanying redness, you should put the following ingredients on your "do *not* use" list—mint (including menthol, menthyl lactate, and peppermint), witch hazel (please stop using witch hazel, it hurts skin—we are frustrated at how often we see it recommended), SD or denatured alcohol, eucalyptus, lemon, lime, grapefruit, vinegar (including apple cider vinegar), essential oils, and fragrance of any kind (whether from essential oils, fragrant plant extracts, or synthetic compounds)—as these will wreak havoc on your skin.

Using oil-absorbing products that cause irritation or overly dry out your skin will not help get rid of acne or stop oil production. You may temporarily have a less greasy appearance on your face and your skin may feel smoother, but the drying effect will lead to more problems. **There are oil-absorbing products that don't cause dryness or irritation and that will still improve the look and feel of your skin; those are the ones to focus on.**

Be sure to remove all of your makeup before going to bed. Makeup in and of itself does not cause acne (there is a special kind of acne called *acne cosmetica*, discussed later in this chapter), but falling asleep with makeup on, or just not getting it all off before bed, reduces skin's ability to exfoliate. This leads to blocked pores, which, in turn, can cause skin to feel dry or rough, and increase acne.

If you need to remove heavy makeup, or just want to feel extra clean, use a cleansing brush with very soft bristles (and we mean very soft), a soft washcloth with a gentle water-soluble cleanser, or a gentle scrub that does not feel rough or scratchy. Rough, abrasive scrubs and cleansing brushes cause micro-tears on skin's surface, which impair skin's ability to heal.

Avoid emollient, creamy moisturizers of any kind. These types of products not only make oily skin feel more oily and greasy, but also can block pores. No matter how you look at it, these products usually are a problem for someone struggling with breakouts and oily skin.

Be careful to keep hair care products off your skin, especially emollient conditioners and heavy styling products. If your hairstyle is such that your hair touches your forehead or the sides of your face, traces of the products you use to style your hair will inevitably end up on your skin. Therefore, if you have acne-prone skin, avoid using thick, waxy hairstyling products along the hairline because they can clog pores and lead to breakouts.

Conditioners can also trigger acne breakouts, so avoid getting these on your face. If you have neck or back acne, try rinsing the conditioner from your hair so that the conditioner does not come into contact with those areas.

Protect yourself from the sun. You might have heard that sunlight can "clear up" or "dry out" acne breakouts, but there is no research indicating that sun exposure (meaning getting a tan or even worse, a sunburn) clears or dries up acne. A tan can make blemishes less noticeable, but it doesn't reduce acne. If anything, unprotected sun exposure weakens skin and makes it unhealthy. Healthy skin can heal and renew itself; perpetually damaged skin has a much harder time repairing itself and eventually stops altogether.

IS YOUR ACNE CAUSED BY STRESS OR HORMONES?

You may have heard that there's a difference between hormonal acne and stress-related acne, but stress is not the cause of acne. Given that just about everyone experiences stress at some point in their life (we don't know anyone who isn't stressed out at some time to one degree or another), then everyone should have acne; obviously, that's not the case.

While stress doesn't cause acne, there does seem to be a connection between stress and breakouts, but only if you already have the genetic trait to have acne. The science behind how stress is related to acne is more theory than fact. Researchers have speculated that a substance in the body known as cortisol (a steroidal hormone everyone has that's produced in excess when you're stressed) may combine with androgens (male hormones, which everyone also has, that are responsible for oil production and most types of acne), which can possibly trigger factors within skin that lead to more breakouts.

What seems certain is that stress releases inflammatory substances in skin that can indeed make acne worse if you already have the genetic tendency to break out. Acne is an inflammatory disorder, so anything that increases inflammation in skin, including stress, can increase the problem.

DOES WEARING MAKEUP CAUSE ACNE?

Wearing makeup does not cause acne—genetics and hormonal balance are the two factors responsible for acne. If wearing makeup caused acne, then everyone who wore makeup would have acne, and that simply isn't the case.

As mentioned previously, breakouts can be caused by emollient or thick products that clog pores. Another cause of breakouts from makeup is not getting it all off every night or, even worse, falling asleep with your makeup on. It isn't unusual to wake up to new breakouts after a night of sleeping in your makeup.

There is a term you may have heard—*acne cosmetica*—that refers to the breakouts some people experience immediately after using a hair care, skin care, or makeup product. Occurring in only a small number of people, it is a sensitizing reaction to the ingredients in the products.

Although acne also might occur after you apply a new makeup product, the breakout might have occurred anyway, especially if it's around the time of your period. That the two coincide is more likely coincidental than a true cause-and-effect reaction, but it takes experimenting to know for sure.

WHAT IF YOU HAVE CYSTIC ACNE?

The most severe type of acne, often referred to as cystic acne, can occur along with mild to moderate acne, where some areas of the face have mild to moderate breakouts and, interspersed or on random occasions, there are deep, painful, cystic acne bumps. Most research indicates that cystic acne is caused by the same factors as mild to moderate acne, but skin has a more extreme response to the triggers. No one knows why someone has cystic acne breakouts rather than the other types of acne. Here's how you know if you have cystic acne:

+ Cystic acne results in raised, swollen, red pimples on the surface of skin that also extend deep under the skin's surface (sometimes referred to as nodules or nodular acne).

+ The pimple may or may not have a "whitehead" showing; no one knows why some cystic breakouts are only large red nodules and not "pimples."

+ Cystic acne is almost always painful to the touch; even when not touched, these bumps can just plain hurt!

+ Because cystic acne bumps are so large and grow deep beneath skin's surface, there is a higher risk of scarring, especially if left untreated or if treated improperly.

Cystic acne almost always requires the attention of a dermatologist because over-the-counter anti-acne products usually are not enough. One thing you can ask your doctor is if you can try over-the-counter salicylic acid–based and benzoyl peroxide–based products to see if they work for you. After trying these options, you and your dermatologist can determine if prescription options are the next step to help you achieve the results you want for your cystic acne. Prescription anti-acne products, used in combination with a great anti-acne skin care routine, can often achieve even better results.

WHAT IF YOU HAVE DRY SKIN AND ACNE?

Dry skin and acne is perhaps one of the most difficult skin issues to treat because the products that are good for dry skin (like emollient moisturizers) can clog pores and make acne worse. It's critically important that you follow all the recommendations for treating acne, but you also need to find hydrating and skin-softening products with fluid or thin lotion textures that eliminate your dry skin without clogging pores. The following list of products recommended for anti-acne and anti-aging includes products that can work brilliantly to reduce acne and treat dry skin as well. You might also need to layer lighter-weight, non-creamy products to get the protection your dry skin needs without triggering acne.

ACNE SOLUTIONS THAT WORK

Research shows that the place to start in treating acne is over-the-counter products that contain BHA (salicylic acid) in concentrations between 0.5% and 2%, and benzoyl peroxide in concentrations between 2.5% and 5%. These two ingredients can work quickly *and* gently to reduce mild to moderate acne, but only if the other ingredients in the products don't irritate skin.

BHA is an amazing multifunctional ingredient that deals with acne in several ways. It not only calms redness and increases hydration to keep the skin healthy and able to heal, but also gently exfoliates the surface of skin to remove built-up layers of dead skin. BHA also exfoliates *inside* the pore, where the pore lining can thicken and prevent the oil from getting out, which makes acne conditions within the pores worse. BHA is truly a multi-tasking superhero ingredient.

For skin care products with BHA to be effective, they must contain a concentration of at least 0.5%; however, for most types of acne a 2% concentration is far more effective. The product's pH is also critical; a pH of 3–4 is optimal. Unfortunately, many BHA products for acne don't meet those criteria—either the concentration of BHA is too low or the pH is too high, or both, so they end up not being very effective, if at all, on acne and clogged pores. BHA products that do meet these criteria are ideal options.

Benzoyl peroxide is considered the most effective over-the-counter choice for managing acne-causing bacteria. Commonly found in concentrations of 2.5% to 5%, benzoyl peroxide goes to work fast to get acne under control. There also are 10% strengths of benzoyl peroxide, but they are considered too irritating and research has shown that they might have side effects (like dry, flaky skin and possibly more breakouts). We recommend starting with a 2.5% concentration applied twice daily and waiting a few weeks to see how your acne responds; then, if you're not seeing the results you want, move to a 5% concentration.

It's interesting to note that benzoyl peroxide was once thought to work only by killing acne-causing bacteria. Recent evidence shows that it also has anti-inflammatory properties, which is great for acne.

If your acne doesn't respond to a 5% concentration of benzoyl peroxide and a 2% BHA exfoliant, there are other options to consider for use along with these ingredients.

Adapalene (form of vitamin A sold under the brand name Differin in North America, where the original 0.1% strength is now available over-the-counter and a 0.3% strength is prescription-only) is a topical gel you can add to your skin care routine and while continuing to use BHA and benzoyl peroxide. There is growing research showing that using adapalene with benzoyl peroxide and BHA can be very effective for acne. There also is research showing that adapalene is a better form of vitamin A to use with benzoyl peroxide because it is more stable than tretinoin (Retin-A and various generics).

If using adapalene, BHA, and benzoyl peroxide doesn't get you the results you want after six to eight weeks of daily use, consult a dermatologist for other topical or oral prescription options. Unfortunately, there are some tenacious forms of acne that do not respond to BHA, benzoyl peroxide, and adapalene. Your doctor may recommend ongoing use of such products, coupled with prescription options, so be sure to follow your doctor's advice.

Keep in mind that one of the major ways to achieve what you want from an anti-acne skin care routine is to be consistent and to use the products everywhere you have acne. Spot-treating acne is almost always a mistake. When you apply anti-acne products only over a new breakout, it might reduce that pimple, but there is no way for you to tell where the next breakouts are going to show up. It's the rare person who gets only one or two breakouts and always in the same spot.

There is no risk to skin from using anti-acne products all over your face. Ongoing, consistent use of anti-acne solutions and an overall healthy skin care routine are absolutely necessary if you want to maintain the results and keep new breakouts from occurring.

DOES SKIN NEED TO PURGE WHEN YOU START USING ANTI-ACNE PRODUCTS?

Skin purging is something many people worry about when they begin using a leave-on BHA exfoliant or other anti-acne products. We understand the concern: It's alarming to see a fresh crop of clogged pores pop up right after you begin using the exfoliant—more breakouts isn't what you expected!

Some people think that such a breakout is just their skin purging the pimples that are hiding beneath the surface, but is that really what's happening? And, if it is, how long does the purge last? Here's what can be happening to your skin if your acne seems to be getting worse before it gets better.

WHAT MAY CAUSE SKIN PURGING?

The theory surrounding skin purging is that when you start using a leave-on exfoliant or other anti-acne products, clogged pores and pimples stuck deep inside the pore are pushed quickly to the surface. Seemingly overnight, a fresh crop of breakouts dots your skin. As the exfoliant takes effect over several days, the purging tapers off and all is well; some think of it as just their skin "getting worse before it gets better."

Such purging does occur for some people, but exactly why remains uncertain. The reasoning about why skin "purges" is that the effective exfoliants and even some of the anti-acne ingredients you start using (such as retinol and benzoyl peroxide) loosen the gunk in the pore and speed cell turnover, thus bringing the clog in the pore to the surface faster.

This makes sense for breakouts that aren't red pimples or acne, meaning they're just flesh-toned clogged pores or blackheads. As salicylic acid penetrates the pore lining, it thins the thick, sticky oil (sebum) buildup as it loosens and reduces the size of the clogs deeper in skin. Salicylic acid also improves the shape of the pore lining and, once the pore is normalized, the backed-up, smaller clog can more easily come to the surface, appearing as a newly clogged pore (blackheads or white bumps—not acne-related pimples).

Most of these clogs would eventually make their way to the surface, but using a product like a BHA exfoliant has the potential to hasten the process. Once on the surface, ongoing use of the BHA continues to eliminate the bump and to shrink the enlarged pores so they are less likely to return.

In terms of purging being about acne (red, swollen pimples), physiologically the premise is faulty. Although improving pore function and killing acne-causing bacteria definitely prevents more pimples from forming, it doesn't cause existing or new pimples to move through the process any faster. Pimples don't come through the pore, even though that's what it looks like.

A pimple forms because, in some instances, the clog in a pore causes the pore lining to rupture, spilling the pore contents—oil, debris, and dead skin—into the surrounding skin. Then, the acne-causing bacteria around and in the pore begin a feeding frenzy. With all of this "food," the bacteria multiply, triggering inflammation that worsens until the body responds by producing a swollen pimple on skin's surface.

IS SKIN PURGING A GOOD THING?

You cannot control whether purging occurs or not. You can skip using a leave-on exfoliant, but that only sets skin up for more trouble down the road, not to mention losing all of the wonderful benefits a BHA exfoliant provides over the long term.

Besides, what you might see on skin's surface after you start using a BHA product would have shown up eventually, or simply would've remained deep in the pore, keeping it clogged and enlarged, and possibly becoming cystic acne. It's actually good to see all this movement, despite the initial distress.

What can also be occurring is that you just happened to start the new product at the same time you would have been going through a new bout of breakouts. This is especially true if you start using new products around the time of your monthly cycle, when all types of breakouts are more common.

Having said that, some people can be sensitive to benzoyl peroxide, salicylic acid, or various retinoids, but a sensitized response does not automatically mean you can't use such ingredients. In such cases, by experimenting with the frequency of use or using one product in the morning and the other at night might get you through the adjustment period.

ARE THERE EFFECTIVE NATURAL ALTERNATIVES FOR TREATING ACNE?

The short answer is: No. While there are many natural ingredients that have amazing benefits for skin (especially in terms of diminishing environmental damage, calming skin, restoring and repairing the layers of skin, and improving hydration), the same just is not true for treating acne. In comparison to benzoyl peroxide, BHA, or over-the-counter adapalene (all of which are synthetic), plant alternatives take a backseat and don't show up at the finish line.

For example, tea tree oil is often touted as a natural option for treating acne, but research that compared it with benzoyl peroxide showed that the tea tree oil didn't perform as well. Plus, the studies used a 5% concentration of tea tree oil, which is far greater than what most skin care products contain. Another issue is that tea tree oil contains many components that are known to be significant allergens capable of triggering irritation.

Witch hazel is in the same category as tea tree oil. Despite what you may have read about witch hazel, it has irritating, drying, and skin-inflaming properties that make acne worse, not better. Yes, there are components of witch hazel that have anti-inflammatory attributes, but they are far outweighed by its extremely astringent, irritating properties. There is also no research showing that witch hazel is helpful for acne.

Coconut oil deserves a bit of explanation because of the strange information we've seen about its benefits for acne. Coconut oil is often mentioned as being good for acne because it is rich in lauric acid, a fatty acid known as a medium-chain triglyceride that's been shown to kill acne-causing bacteria. While that does sound helpful, it also presents problems because it makes skin feel greasy, blocks oil from flowing out of the pore, and, depending on the type of coconut oil, increases inflammation. You can kill acne-causing bacteria without making skin feel more greasy or increasing other problems. We know coconut oil sounds all natural and wonderful—and it is wonderful if you have dry skin—but unless the research shows that it works for acne (and in this case, it doesn't), then it isn't good for those with acne-prone skin.

There are studies showing that some plant extracts can have efficacy against acne, but these studies rarely analyze the performance of the ingredient in a formulation as opposed to just the pure form of the plant extract, or the study looked at how the plant extract worked in the lab (in vitro) as opposed to on people (in vivo). Such studies rarely compare the efficacy of the natural alternatives to the efficacy of benzoyl peroxide, BHA, or over-the-counter adapalene or any of the various prescription options available to treat acne.

Particularly frustrating are studies about natural alternatives to treat acne that are highly questionable—science gone bad! There are many examples, but a recent study really proves the point. The headline was "Natural extracts outweigh synthetic antibiotics for acne treatment" (there's that scary word, "synthetic"). The study assessed the anti-acne benefits of a cream that contained propolis (resinous substance from a beehive), tea tree oil, and aloe vera with the benefits of a cream that contained 3% erythromycin (a prescription antibiotic). The study resoundingly claimed that the natural product worked better than the prescription product. What the study did not mention, however, is that erythromycin is considered obsolete as a prescription for treating acne, especially in comparison to many other options, such as the antibiotic clindamycin combined with benzoyl peroxide, or a BHA product combined with a benzoyl peroxide product. The study should have compared the results with the results of the newer options; it then would have been far more relevant and meaningful.

TREATING BACK ACNE (BACNE) & NECK ACNE

It's well known that back and neck acne can be very different from acne on the face, but no one knows why. Breakouts on the back and neck are frequently deeper, larger, more painful, and take longer to form a pimple (whitehead) so you can safely pop it. And, overall, acne on the back and neck generally takes longer to go away, even with the best anti-acne products.

Although there is a general qualitative difference between acne on the face and acne on the neck and back, the underlying causes and treatment are the same. The exact same skin care dos and don'ts apply, as do which over-the-counter products to use and when to see a physician about acne from the neck down.

What about using **acne body washes** that contain benzoyl peroxide or salicylic acid? While those can be helpful in some cases, research has shown that both ingredients work best—especially for stubborn acne—when left on skin rather than rinsed off. But, don't leave a cleanser with BHA or benzoyl peroxide on the skin in hopes of having the active ingredients absorb better because the cleansing ingredients in these products are too drying and potentially irritating when left on for longer than necessary.

THE ANTI-ACNE DIET

Diet is rarely the cause of acne unless you are allergic or have a sensitizing reaction to certain foods. Such cases are usually an individual reaction and not randomized to most people. However, if you happen to be allergic to nuts, shellfish, other fish, gluten, or lactose, you may find that when you stop eating those foods your acne breakouts lessen and sometimes even go away.

What we do know from research is that eating a healthy, anti-inflammatory diet is great for your body and can also help diminish breakouts. Because acne is an inflammatory disorder, it's been shown that anything you do to calm inflammation in your body benefits your skin as well. Less inflammation in your system can result in fewer breakouts.

Here's what the science says about some of the most common food groups that are thought to cause acne—some are nothing more than myths, while others have been shown to increase breakouts for those already struggling with the problem:

Fried, greasy foods are often blamed for blemishes. But, contrary to this decades-old belief, eating greasy food doesn't seem to affect acne or oil production. Excess oils in your diet don't flow out through your pores; they're either stored elsewhere in the body or excreted normally.

Consuming good fats like omega fatty acids and oils found in fish, seeds, and nuts is known to reduce inflammation and can be a wonderful addition to a healthy diet. On the other hand, bad fats that increase inflammation in the body (saturated fats) are similarly bad for skin and should be avoided.

Another common belief is that **chocolate** can lead to breakouts. Pure chocolate (cocoa) is a powerful antioxidant and, therefore, has the potential to reduce inflammation in the body. But, you're not going to derive that wonderful benefit when the chocolate also contains inflammation-causing ingredients like sugar, butter, flour (gluten), or other starches.

A growing amount of research suggests that consuming **dairy products**, especially high-fat dairy products or dairy products loaded with sugar, such as milk, cheese, and yogurt, can have a negative impact on the severity and frequency of acne breakouts. Some studies point to a connection with lactose or the natural hormones found in dairy products (yes, even the organic and grass-fed types), but it isn't 100% clear why this reaction to dairy products occurs for those who tend to break out.

Relatively recent research has pointed to a low-glycemic diet being helpful for improving acne. A low-glycemic diet refers to different types of foods and the amount of carbohydrates they contain. While carbohydrates are important for your health, which ones you eat can have either a negative or positive impact on your body. The purpose of a glycemic index (GI) diet is to eat carbohydrate-containing foods that are less likely to cause rapid increases (spikes) in your blood sugar levels. High blood sugar triggers excess insulin, leading to widespread inflammation within the body, among other health issues.

Regardless of what the food is, if you want to find out if it is making your acne worse, the solution is simple: Either stop eating the suspect food or greatly reduce the amount of it you eat and see how your skin is doing after about four to six weeks. You might see a noticeable difference, or you might notice no change at all, but that's the best way to find out what works for you.

How the skin's microbiome—the balance of good and bad bacteria, among other micro-organisms that reside naturally on skin—can affect acne is discussed in Chapter 17.

HOW TO POP A PIMPLE

Most of us have been there: When you have a red, swollen pimple with a glaring whitehead in the center, it's natural to want to pop it! Unfortunately, even a great skin care routine that reduces acne breakouts doesn't mean you still won't get occasional, or even regular, breakouts (though hopefully far less frequently and less severe than before).

What you do with that pimple to diminish its appearance and speed up its disappearance is as important as using the right products. In other words, it's perfectly okay to pop a pimple. What's crucial is *how* you do it, because the wrong approach could cause damage or, even worse, scarring.

We're sure you've read that you should *never* pop a pimple, and we understand the concern— you really can hurt skin if you don't pop a pimple **the right way** *and* if it's not **the right kind** of pimple to pop. Over-squeezing and aggressive pushing, picking, or puncturing can cause serious damage that can last far longer than your zit would have—possibly permanently.

However, if you carefully pop a pimple by following the steps below, it can actually be beneficial. You'll find that the pimple goes away faster and heals better than if you just leave it alone.

The basic starting point is all in the timing: You need to know when the offending blemish is ready for its contents to be released. How can you tell? You'll know it's ready when you see a noticeable "whitehead" showing up on the surface and the zit begins to feel, as well as look, swollen.

If you don't see a whitehead, abort the mission. Trying to pop a pimple that isn't ready will do more harm than good; this is especially true for deep, large bumps, such as with cystic acne. When the time is right, you must be as gentle as humanly possible. Here are the steps to follow to pop a pimple the right way:

1. Buy a comedone extractor.
2. Cleanse your face with a gentle, water-soluble cleanser and a soft washcloth or a gentle scrub. Do NOT use cold or hot water, as both will increase redness and make acne worse.
3. Dry your skin gently. Do not use the comedone extractor or squeeze when your skin is wet because it's more vulnerable to tearing and might leave a lingering sore.
4. Center the comedone extractor's opening over the pimple. Then gently (and we mean gently), and with very little pressure (and we mean VERY little pressure), push the comedone extractor down on the whitehead and move it across the bump. That should release its "contents." And yes, this part can be gross.
5. You may have to repeat step 4 one or two times, but that's all, stop right there. Going further can easily damage the skin and worsen the breakout.
6. Remember to be gentle; the goal is to remove the whitehead without creating a scab or damaging the surrounding skin because doing so might cause scarring.
7. Afterward, follow up with the rest of your skin care routine.

RECOMMENDED PRODUCTS FROM PAULA'S CHOICE SKINCARE FOR ACNE-PRONE SKIN

Cleanser
+ **CLEAR Pore Normalizing Cleanser**

Exfoliant
+ **CLEAR Regular Strength Anti-Redness Exfoliating Solution with 2% Salicylic Acid** (for mild to moderate acne)
+ **CLEAR Extra Strength Anti-Redness Exfoliating Solution with 2% Salicylic Acid** (for moderate to stubborn acne)
+ **CLEAR Acne Body Spray**

Booster
+ **1% Retinol Booster**
+ **10% Niacinamide Booster**
+ **10% Azelaic Acid Booster**

Treatment
+ **CLEAR Regular Strength Daily Skin Clearing Treatment with 2.5% Benzoyl Peroxide** (for mild to moderate acne)
+ **CLEAR Extra Strength Daily Skin Clearing Treatment with 5% Benzoyl Peroxide** (for moderate to stubborn acne)
+ **CBD Oil + Retinol** (for acne and dry skin)

Mask
+ **CLEAR Purifying Clay Mask**

Sunscreen
+ **CLEAR Ultra-light Daily Hydrating Fluid SPF 30**

Moisturizer
+ **CLEAR Oil-Free Moisturizer**
+ **Water-Infusing Electrolyte Moisturizer** (all skin types)
+ **Probiotic Nutrient Moisturizer** (all skin types)

RECOMMENDED PRODUCTS FROM PAULA'S CHOICE SKINCARE FOR ACNE-PRONE SKIN AND ANTI-AGING

Cleanser
+ **RESIST Perfectly Balanced Foaming Cleanser**

Exfoliant
+ **CLEAR Regular Strength Anti-Redness Exfoliating Solution with 2% Salicylic Acid** (for mild to moderate acne)
+ **CLEAR Extra Strength Anti-Redness Exfoliating Solution with 2% Salicylic Acid** (for moderate to stubborn acne)
+ **RESIST Advanced Pore-Refining Treatment 4% BHA** (to alternate or layer with one of the CLEAR exfoliants above)

Serum
+ **RESIST Ultra-Light Super Antioxidant Concentrate Serum**
+ **SKIN BALANCING Super Antioxidant Concentrate Serum with Retinol**

Booster
+ **1% Retinol Booster**
+ **10% Niacinamide Booster**
+ **10% Azelaic Acid Booster**
+ **C15 Super Booster**

Treatment
+ **CLEAR Regular Strength Daily Skin Clearing Treatment with 2.5% Benzoyl Peroxide** (for mild to moderate acne)
+ **CLEAR Extra Strength Daily Skin Clearing Treatment with 5% Benzoyl Peroxide** (for moderate to stubborn acne)
+ **CLEAR Acne Body Spray**
+ **CLINICAL 20% Niacinamide Treatment**
+ **CBD Oil + Retinol** (for acne and dry skin)

Mask
+ **RADIANCE Renewal Mask**
+ **CLEAR Purifying Mask**

Eye Cream or Eye Gel
+ **RESIST Anti-Aging Eye Gel**
+ **CLINICAL Ceramide-Enriched Firming Eye Cream**

Sunscreen
+ RESIST Super-Light Daily Wrinkle Defense SPF 30
+ CLEAR Ultra-light Daily Hydrating Fluid SPF 30

Moisturizer
+ RESIST Anti-Aging Clear Skin Hydrator
+ DEFENSE Nightly Reconditioning Moisturizer
+ Water-Infusing Electrolyte Moisturizer
+ Probiotic Nutrient Moisturizer

CHAPTER 13

HOW TO FADE POST-ACNE RED OR BROWN MARKS

WHAT CAUSES POST-ACNE HYPERPIGMENTATION MARKS?

As a pimple starts to form, it almost immediately begins to damage skin in the process. The swelling, inflammation, and whitish-colored pus a pimple causes, in the pore as well as in the lower and upper layers, damages skin.

When the pimple starts to heal, the inflammation can linger. This causes a noticeable pink to dark brown mark where the pimple used to be, known as post-inflammatory hyperpigmentation (PIH). If you have a fair to medium skin tone, you'll most likely see pink to red or even purple-tinged post-acne marks; if you have a medium to very dark skin tone, you will likely see tan to dark brown or black post-acne marks.

Although post-acne marks can linger long after the blemish has gone away, there are ways to reduce the amount of time they hang around. Worth noting: If you haven't repeatedly picked or overly squeezed the blemish and caused scabs, the leftover marks are unlikely to be permanent.

REDUCE THE RISK OF POST-ACNE MARKS BEFORE THEY HAPPEN

Don't create scabs by over-squeezing or picking at your skin. We want to stress how incredibly important it is to never create scabs by picking or over-squeezing pimples. Every blemish doesn't necessarily end up with a post-acne mark, but it will certainly leave one if you wound skin and cause a scab to form. How you treat a pimple when it shows up can make all the difference in the world in how it heals and how long a post-acne mark will last.

The same skin care routine we discussed in the previous chapter on treating acne is your first line of defense to help minimize the occurrence of post-acne marks and get rid of them faster.

Sun protection is non-negotiable. Regardless of your skin color, unprotected sun exposure damages skin and prevents healing. We know it's not easy when you have acne-prone skin to believe that wearing a sunscreen won't make you break out, but there is no way around the need for it. It's truly worth the effort to find an option you'll want to apply every day, but it doesn't have to be what you think of as a traditional sunscreen. Foundations with SPF 30 or greater are a great way to get sun protection for your face. If you apply the foundation liberally (meaning more coverage), you can avoid the need to use a lotion-textured sunscreen that many people with acne don't like on their skin. Just don't forget to apply a regular sunscreen to your neck and chest!

STOP tanning, whether in the sun or in tanning beds. While tanned skin might help minimize the contrast between your skin and the PIH marks and make new breakouts less obvious, the damage from tanning impairs skin's ability to heal, which means the post-acne marks will stick around even longer. As we've stated repeatedly throughout this book, sun damage harms skin in numerous ways, including increasing the time it takes for post-acne marks to heal.

Use additional skin care products loaded with skin-restoring ingredients, antioxidants, anti-redness ingredients, and skin-replenishing ingredients. These essential ingredients, which we discuss throughout this book, are important for all skin types and are essential for healing post-acne marks. Research makes it clear that these ingredients help skin recover from the damage a pimple causes, along with providing other benefits. When the products you use contain these ingredients and do not contain pore-clogging ingredients or make skin feel greasy and oily, you have the perfect solution for diminishing the appearance of red bumps and post-acne marks. For best results, choose only products with lightweight lotion, liquid, gel, or thin serum textures.

TREATMENT FOR POST-ACNE MARKS

The inflammation that causes post-acne marks is the same for everyone; what differs is how they appear on the surface of skin, which depends on skin color. For those with lighter skin tones, post-acne marks are usually pink to red. For those with medium to dark brown skin tones, post-acne marks are usually brown to black, which is because people with darker skin tones naturally have more melanin in their skin and inflammation increases melanin production, causing the post-acne marks to be brown to black in color.

Regardless of the color, the basic treatment for healing post-acne marks is the same for everyone. The most important step is to reduce the leftover inflammation.

What complicates matters is when post-acne marks are brown or black; they tend to be harder to resolve and often require extra treatment products. A combination of products with anti-redness (anti-inflammatory) ingredients as well as products with melanin-inhibiting ingredients can be a powerful combination.

Regardless of skin color, sunscreen is still the first line of defense for helping to lessen the discoloration of post-acne marks. Along with sunscreen, the research shows that the best ingredients for inhibiting post-acne discolorations are azelaic acid, salicylic acid, licorice extract, retinol, vitamin C, niacinamide, and certain peptides.

RECOMMENDED PRODUCTS FROM PAULA'S CHOICE SKINCARE FOR POST-ACNE RED, BROWN, OR BLACK MARKS FOR ALL SKIN TYPES

(Follow the list of recommended products in the previous chapter on treating acne. The products below are add-ons to help calm and repair the damage and discoloration left over from a pimple):

Booster
+ **10% Azelaic Acid Booster**
+ **10% Niacinamide Booster**
+ **1% Retinol Booster**
+ **C25 Super Booster**

Serum
+ **RESIST Ultra-light Super Antioxidant Concentrate Serum**

Treatment
+ **CLINICAL Triple Action Dark Spot Eraser Gel with 2% BHA and 2% Hydroquinone**
+ **CLINICAL 20% Niacinamide Treatment**
+ **CLINICAL 0.3% Retinol + 2% Bakuchiol Treatment**

Serum
+ **RESIST Ultra-light Super Antioxidant Concentrate Serum** (for normal to oily skin)

Mask
+ **RADIANCE Renewal Mask**

CHAPTER 14

FADING UNEVEN SKIN TONE AND DARK BROWN SPOTS

WHAT CAUSES BROWN SPOTS AND UNEVEN SKIN TONE?

Brown spots and uneven skin tone are frustrating, but the answer is simple: These discolorations are caused primarily by repeated, unprotected exposure to daylight. Dark brown spots are localized buildups of melanin that begin in the lower layers of skin when we're young. You don't see them until they make their way to the surface (this can take years). Left untreated, they become more and more pronounced over time, but, luckily, there are products that can offer significant improvement.

Some excess melanin production can be caused by hormones (particularly during pregnancy or from taking birth control pills). This type of uneven skin tone appears as large patches of light brown areas, generally on the sides of the face, but they can appear anywhere on the face.

Melanin is the general term for the pigments in skin responsible for its color. Uneven skin tone refers to a change in the overall color appearance of your skin caused in the exact same way dark or ashy brown spots are caused. It's just that for uneven skin tone, the discoloration is diffuse rather than concentrated in one area. Not surprisingly, most people with sun damage struggle with both concerns at the same time.

Strangely enough, back in the day, dark brown spots used to be called liver spots, even though they had nothing to do with the liver. Today they're often referred to as age spots even though they have nothing to do with how old you are. Dark brown spots and uneven skin tone are all about the amount of unprotected sun exposure you've accumulated over the years. The discolorations (and a tan in general) are your skin's damage response to being exposed to daylight without sun protection.

Check it out: The parts of your body that are usually hidden from the sun will have minimal to no brown discolorations and the skin tone in those areas will be even and normal. In contrast, the parts of your body that see daylight without protection will have uneven skin color and the dark brown spots will become bigger and more noticeable every year. But, you can stop this from happening if you are dedicated to following the recommendations we present in this chapter.

IMPROVEMENT BEGINS WITH SUNSCREEN!

Without question, the first line of defense is sun-smart behavior, which means avoiding direct exposure to daylight (seeking shade, wearing sunglasses, a hat, UPF-rated protective clothing) and using a sunscreen with SPF 30 or greater daily (365 days a year, rain or shine), and reapplying when needed.

Diligent use of a sunscreen is the core step of any skin care routine, but even more so for someone who already has an uneven skin tone or has developed dark brown spots. There's simply no room for compromise: Sun protection, skin lighteners, and skin brighteners are a package deal. When it comes to improving uneven skin tone or dark brown discolorations, one cannot work effectively without the others.

Stated bluntly: If you don't diligently avoid sun exposure and use sunscreen, along with applying skin-lightening or skin-brightening products, don't blame the latter for not working. Even the best skin lighteners and skin brighteners can't keep up with the ongoing damage.

IMPROVING SKIN DISCOLORATION CAUSED BY SUN DAMAGE

For over 50 years research has consistently shown the most effective ingredient for reducing skin discolorations caused by sun damage is hydroquinone in concentrations of 2% to 4%. In the United States, 2% concentrations of hydroquinone are available over-the-counter, while 4% concentrations are available only by prescription.

Despite hydroquinone being well-established in dozens of studies as the gold standard for fading skin discolorations caused by sun damage, it also has a controversial reputation that makes many people nervous about using it. However, a closer look at the research reveals a different picture. There are decades of studies showing how effective hydroquinone is and a comparative lack of evidence showing it is dangerous for skin. You might very well still not want to use products that contain hydroquinone, so it's good to know there are alternatives with encouraging research behind them, though not as longstanding as hydroquinone.

What can be an extremely rare side effect of using hydroquinone is its association with a condition called exogenous ochronosis (skin darkening) when used in high concentrations (greater than what's approved for sale over-the-counter). It's interesting to point out that exogenous ochronosis is also a genetic disorder that can occur regardless of what you apply to skin.

GETTING THE BEST RESULTS FROM HYDROQUINONE

When used once or twice daily, along with daily application of a sunscreen, you can expect hydroquinone to lighten and possibly completely fade some brown and dark spots, typically in about two to three months. You will see some improvement sooner than that, but for optimal results you must be patient; remember, these spots took time to form, so they're not going to go away overnight.

Once you reach the level of improvement you were hoping for, you can reduce the frequency of application to once a day to maintain results. You cannot cut back on the frequency of applying sunscreen, but you can reduce the frequency of application of your skin-lightening product.

Your hydroquinone product must be packaged in opaque packaging that minimizes exposure to light and air. Hydroquinone is not an air-stable ingredient; it degrades on exposure to air, which means it should not be packaged in a jar because once the jar is opened, it lets air in, which eventually makes the hydroquinone lose its effectiveness and, ironically, causes the product to become brown.

You can use hydroquinone-based lightening products as part of your skin care routine. It is considered a treatment step and would fit in after cleansing, toning, and applying your leave-on AHA or BHA exfoliant.

After you apply your exfoliant, all other products are applied in an order that depends on how fluid or how thick they are—the more fluid products go on first and the thicker products follow. During the day, the last skin care product you apply is your sunscreen. Never apply any other skin care product over your sunscreen to avoid diluting it.

SKIN-BRIGHTENING OPTIONS

Natural alternatives for skin-brightening abound, with research pointing to a handful of fairly well-known, established ingredients, such as: *Mitracarpus scaber* (madder) extract, *Uva ursi* (bearberry) extract, *Morus bombycis* extract (mulberry), *Morus alba* extract (white mulberry), *Broussonetia papyrifera* extract (paper mulberry), and whole plant or components of *Glycyrrhiza glabra* (licorice). Other research-supported brightening ingredients include high concentrations of niacinamide (vitamin B3), high concentrations of vitamin C (usually ascorbic acid, but other forms also have evidence of efficacy), arbutin, 2-5% tranexamic acid (a synthetic amino acid), 10% azelaic acid (derived from grains, although the final cosmetic ingredient is considered synthetic), and ellagic acid (derived from nuts, pomegranate, and berries).

These are all good options to consider as skin-brightening ingredients. It's even better when they are combined in a single product if the goal is to prevent changes in skin tone. If you have advanced signs of discoloration, you might need products with higher concentrations to get the best results. For example, a 10% niacinamide product, 10% azelaic acid product, and a 15% to 25% vitamin C product, when layered one over the other in the morning and one at night, can be very effective.

In terms of the plant extracts mentioned above and arbutin, it is interesting to note that these extracts, when absorbed into skin, break down to hydroquinone, which explains why they can have a positive effect. Isn't it ironic that hydroquinone is a natural component of many plants?

WHAT TO EXPECT FROM USING A SKIN BRIGHTENER

The desired result from a skin brightener is to see brighter, more even-toned, radiant-looking skin. With once- or twice-daily use of a well-formulated skin brightener (containing the ingredients mentioned above) and diligent daily use of a sunscreen, you can progressively get relatively close to the results you want. Of course, to a large degree, it depends on how advanced the problem was when you started.

Be sure to keep in mind that the brightening won't happen overnight. We completely understand the desire to see immediate improvement, but it took several years of ongoing daylight exposure for the dullness and uneven skin tone to show up on the surface, so, it stands to reason that you need to be patient and persistent as you wait for them to fade.

If you want results from a skin-brightening product, you need to use it every day, morning and evening, along with daily application of a sunscreen rated SPF 30 or greater for at least three months before you'll see significant results. Some people see results sooner, but maximum improvement and continued maintenance is a commitment to using these products regularly. None of these products are a cure.

You can start using skin-brightening products as soon as you decide you want to combat the effect that sun damage has had on your skin tone. If you haven't been good about sun protection, the discolorations are already there, below the surface, by your early 20s! According to the CDC (Centers for Disease Control and Prevention), most people don't use sunscreen daily and don't apply it adequately. While nowadays more adults use sunscreen when they're outside, at least during the summer, less than 15% of teens and young adults do. Unfortunately, it is the cumulative daily exposure throughout the entire year—that is, 365 days a year—that is relevant to skin cancer, skin aging, and overall skin health. It is not just about exposure during the warm summer months or when you're on vacation in a sunny climate, but also about exposure during the winter, when most people don't use sunscreen consistently.

Depending on the amount, size, and depth of your uneven skin tone, you'll most likely need more than one skin-brightening product. Each skin-brightening ingredient works on a different pathway in skin to inhibit and minimize how much abnormal melanin is produced. Going after more than one path with a combination of effective ingredients is the best way to get results. This can be as simple as using one type of brightening product during the day and a different formula at night.

RECOMMENDED PRODUCTS FROM PAULA'S CHOICE SKINCARE FOR SKIN LIGHTENING FOR ALL SKIN TYPES YOU CAN ADD TO YOUR SKIN CARE ROUTINE

Treatment
+ CLINICAL Triple Action Dark Spot Eraser 2% BHA AND 2% Hydroquinone Gel
+ CLINICAL Triple Action Dark Spot Eraser 7% AHA and 2% Hydroquinone Lotion

Sunscreen
+ RESIST Super-Light Daily Wrinkle Defense SPF 30 (normal to oily skin)
+ RESIST Youth-Extending Daily Hydrating Fluid SPF 50 (normal to oily skin)
+ DEFENSE Essential Glow Moisturizer SPF 50 (all skin types)
+ SKIN RECOVERY Daily Moisturizing Lotion SPF 30 (normal to dry skin)
+ SKIN BALANCING Ultra-Sheer Daily Defense SPF 30 (normal to oily skin)
+ CALM Mineral Moisturizer SPF 30 Normal to Dry Skin
+ CALM Mineral Moisturizer SPF 30 Normal to Oily Skin

RECOMMENDED PRODUCTS FROM PAULA'S CHOICE SKINCARE FOR SKIN BRIGHTENING FOR ALL SKIN TYPES YOU CAN ADD TO YOUR SKIN CARE ROUTINE

Booster
+ 10% Niacinamide Booster
+ C15 or C25 Super Boosters (C25 is great for stubborn spots)
+ 10% Azelaic Acid Booster

Treatment
+ CLINICAL 1% Retinol Treatment
+ CLINICAL 20% Niacinamide Treatment

Mask
+ RADIANCE Renewal Mask

Sunscreen
+ RESIST Super-Light Daily Wrinkle Defense SPF 30 (all skin types)
+ RESIST Youth-Extending Daily Fluid SPF 50 (normal to oily skin)
+ SKIN RECOVERY Daily Moisturizing Lotion SPF 30 (normal to dry skin)
+ SKIN BALANCING Ultra-Sheer Daily Defense SPF 30 (normal to oily skin)
+ CALM Mineral Moisturizer SPF 30 Normal to Dry Skin
+ CALM Mineral Moisturizer SPF 30 Normal to Oily Skin

CHAPTER 15

THE TRUTH ABOUT PUFFY EYES AND DARK CIRCLES

IF YOU DO WHAT YOU'VE ALWAYS DONE...

You will always get what you always got. That's a basic fact of life; sometimes the things you've done are good for you and sometimes they aren't. When it comes to your eye area, you will need to make certain changes you haven't considered before to get the best results. The trouble is that many people are reluctant to change, especially when the change doesn't involve a magic eye product.

None of what you're about to read is a miracle solution, but don't let that deter you because there's a lot you can do to reduce dark circles and puffy eyes. What makes the information somewhat lackluster is that the research and data about what you can do to treat puffy eyes and dark circles hasn't changed much in the past 10 years. There are still limitations on the amount of improvement that skin care and lifestyle changes can offer.

Having said that, what *is* remarkable and dramatic are the studies about the impact superhero ingredients (we discuss those in the next chapter) can have when used around the eye area. The surprise? Many products for the eye area don't contain these superhero ingredients—and they should!

Lifestyle changes also can make a difference, although many people don't change what they're doing and then wonder why they still have the problem. If you follow our recommendations below, we can guarantee you'll get the best results possible. The catch? You need to do all of it. One product is never enough, and one lifestyle change won't be enough, either.

CAN YOU GET RID OF PUFFY EYES?

Puffy eyes are a common problem for lots of people because there are so many factors that can cause them. Some people wake up with puffy eyes, but then the puffiness decreases or goes away after their morning skin care routine. Some people have puffy eyes intermittently during the day (often associated with consuming too much alcohol or salt the night before, or not getting enough sleep). And some people just have puffy eyes all the time. Each situation presents unique challenges. We suspect that no matter what products you've tried you're still hoping for better outcomes. The question is: Why? The answers are enlightening.

The kind of results you can achieve depends on the reasons why your eye area is puffy. For some people, puffy eyes are the natural appearance of their eye area based on inherited traits. For others, a major cause of puffy eyes is that the fat pads under the eye shift and move through muscles and skin that have become flaccid due to sun damage, age, and gravity. The fat pads then protrude into pockets of skin, resulting in puffy eyes, often referred to as under-eye bags. This can begin to happen in your early 30s, becoming more pronounced with each decade.

If your puffy eyes are an inherited trait or a result of fat pad movement around the eye area, the only way to make it go away is with procedures performed by a cosmetic dermatologist or surgeon. That's a decision worth considering because skin care products can't help in this situation. In a short period of time, you can spend a small fortune on ineffective products, when that money might be better spent on procedures proven to work.

If your eye area is puffy for reasons other than inherited traits or fat pads pouching through skin, then lifestyle choices along with skin care products can have a considerable impact. Such products can even lead to good results on inherited or fat pad–generated puffy eyes—just not as much.

Here's what you can do to reduce puffy eyes; again, skin care products alone can't do the entire job:

1. **Sleep position:** Keeping your head flat while you sleep allows fluid to collect in the skin around your eyes. Sleeping with your head slightly elevated (making sure your neck is properly supported) can help limit fluid retention in the eye area. Gentle fingertip tapping around the eye when you wake up also can help with this kind of swelling. Do not massage the skin around your eyes. Pulling at the skin anywhere on the face causes it to sag by stretching skin's elastin fibers, which are what enable it to bounce back into place.

2. **Diet:** Alcohol consumption and a diet high in salt leads to water retention and increased puffiness around the eyes, which can linger throughout the day. Moderating or limiting your intake of alcohol, sodium, and processed foods can be incredibly helpful, as can adding antioxidant-rich foods to your diet (e.g., fruits, vegetables, salmon). All of these can make a HUGE difference, not only in how your eye area looks, but also in how you feel!

3. **Contact lenses:** Even under the best of circumstances, contact lenses can cause your eyes to feel irritated and look puffy. Ensure you are wearing the most comfortable type of contacts for your vision correction. Follow your eye-care provider's exact recommendations for cleansing, wear, and disposal. Keeping your eyes lubricated with appropriate eye drops is also helpful.

4. **Allergies:** Exposure to allergens, either in the air or by rubbing your eyes with allergen-laced fingers (touching plants or animals you're allergic to and then touching your eyes will transfer the allergen) can contribute to perpetual puffiness. Talk to your physician or consult your pharmacist about taking an antihistamine or using anti-allergy eye drops to control allergy symptoms such as runny, itchy eyes. This issue is far more prevalent than most people think.

5. **Dry skin:** Dryness around your eyes can cause sensitivity and a heavier, crepey appearance that makes puffy eyes look lined, tired, and less taut. An eye cream with skin-replenishing ingredients that hydrate skin, skin-restoring ingredients to repair damage and strengthen skin, and antioxidants to reduce environmental damage (air pollution is an undeniable problem for eyes) will keep skin substantially softened, smoothed, and soothed. It can often make an immediate visible improvement.

6. **Makeup left on overnight:** Falling asleep in your makeup or not removing every trace of it when you cleanse your face irritates skin and can cause eyes to be puffy! Be sure to meticulously remove your makeup every night with a gentle, fragrance-free cleanser and then remove the last traces of eye makeup with an equally gentle makeup remover (one that's also colorant-free is best for the eye area; you don't need a blue or pink eye makeup remover). Remember: Do not rub or pull the skin around your eyes when removing your makeup so you don't help gravity increase sagging of the skin and muscles around the eyes or face.

7. **Exposure to harsh Ingredients:** Ingredients like menthol, camphor, SD or denatured alcohol, essential oils, fragrant plant extracts, or any kind of fragrance (whether essential oils, fragrant plant extracts, or synthetic sources) shouldn't come anywhere close to your eyes. Makeup or skin care products that contain such ingredients can cause eyes to be puffy and make the situation worse.

8. **Sun protection:** You can't avoid the endless problems that unprotected sun exposure causes for skin anywhere on the face. It's not just bad for eye-area skin, it's terribly harmful to the eye itself—just ask your ophthalmologist. An eye cream or well-formulated moisturizer with SPF 30 or greater is critical to prevent premature aging of skin in the eye area. Sun protection also can help get puffiness under control to a certain extent. It's even more critical for improving dark circles, but more about that in the next section. For the eye area, it's preferable to use only mineral-based sunscreens, which contain only titanium dioxide and/or zinc oxide as the active ingredients. It's not that synthetic sunscreen ingredients aren't effective, it's that they have a slight tendency to be sensitizing around the eyes, while the pure mineral sunscreen ingredients are rarely, if ever, sensitizing.

9. **Sunglasses:** Wearing sunglasses is important in several ways for having healthy eyes, as routine exposure to daylight causes macular degeneration (a condition that impairs vision). UV-protecting sunglasses are the perfect adjunct to wearing sunscreen because they substantially increase sun protection. This, in turn, keeps the skin around your eyes young and healthy, which includes diminishing puffy eyes. If you don't damage skin around your eyes, the structure of skin will remain strong and resilient, possibly even preventing puffy eyes.

While the solutions above may not be as extraordinary as you had hoped (we get it—we wish eye creams could magically get rid of all puffiness as much as you do), you now have the truth. No more wasting money on products that can't work as claimed. Homing in on the cause of your puffy eyes, adapting healthy lifestyle changes and habits, and then applying the best eye creams or gels and sunscreens can add up to beautiful results.

CAN YOU LIGHTEN DARK CIRCLES UNDER THE EYE?

Shadows and dark circles under the eye are caused by several factors. Some can be addressed by using the right skin care products, but there are some dark circles that skin care can't address, at least not as much as we want. That's why product after product you've used in hopes they would eliminate dark circles haven't made the difference you anticipated. This is our hype-free list (the truth, the whole truth, and nothing but the truth) of the causes and solutions for this common, yet still frustrating, cosmetic problem.

Numerous factors can cause or worsen dark circles, including:
1. Unprotected sun exposure increases the production of melanin, the brown pigment in skin. Increasing the production of brown pigment around the eyes either creates dark circles or makes the dark circles you already have darker.
2. Prominent purple-blue veins near the surface of skin under the eye can cause the area to look dark because skin is very thin in that area.
3. Allergies and the resulting constant rubbing at your eyes not only causes skin around the eye to eventually sag, but also can create a dark, ashy appearance under the eye.
4. Genetics might predispose you to having deeper skin tone around or under the eye area.
5. Natural shadows can occur as a result of deep-set eyes or shadows can be caused by skin under the eyes beginning to sag.
6. Built-up dead skin around the eye that doesn't shed naturally leaves a thicker layer, resulting in a dehydrated, dull appearance that can appear dark or ashy.

What follows are the best things you can do to start improving the appearance of dark circles.

Every day, use a moisturizer or eye cream with sunscreen of SPF 30 or greater that contains only zinc oxide and/or titanium dioxide as the active ingredients. These two sunscreen ingredients are exceptionally gentle and are best for the eye area because skin in that area is easily irritated. It also is helpful if the product has a luminous finish to deliver a light-reflective effect that helps offset the dark circles.

Apply your AHA or BHA leave-on exfoliant just around the outside of the eye area, but not near the lash line or the eyelid. Gentle exfoliation can make a difference overnight in the smoothness and radiance of the under-eye area, making it look brighter and less ashy.

Apply an emollient eye cream or moisturizer around the eyes at night to keep skin super hydrated and softened. The product also should contain skin-restoring ingredients and antioxidants to protect from environmental damage, to help strengthen the surface of skin, and to shore up the support layers below. Those ingredients can make a difference in every aspect of skin around your eyes.

Twice daily, apply a well-formulated brightening product with multiple brightening ingredients, such as niacinamide or azelaic acid. Keep in mind, not everyone can use high concentrations of bio-active ingredients around their eyes, but because these can produce such impressive results, they're worth testing to see if they work for you.

Use a great concealer as part of your makeup routine. When all is said and done, depending on the type of dark circles you have, skin care has its limitations. That's where a concealer comes to the rescue. The color of the concealer must be light enough to cover the circles convincingly, but not so light that it gives the appearance of a white mask around your eyes. Color-correcting concealers such as those that are strongly peach, orange, or other non-skin colors can mask the circles, but you'll most likely need another concealer to completely cover their appearance.

Consider using an antihistamine. Allergies can be a major cause of dark circles and puffy eyes, but most people don't even know they have allergies. Research indicates that more than 50% of the world's population has allergies that affect the sinuses. This directly affects swelling and potential darkening in the eye area. Talk to your doctor or pharmacist about over-the-counter and prescription allergy medication options.

Wear UV-rated sunglasses to increase protection for the delicate skin around the eye and to protect your vision. Make sure they extend past the lower eye area and, preferably, have wide side pieces to block UV light coming in through the sides.

RECOMMENDED PRODUCTS FROM PAULA'S CHOICE SKINCARE FOR ALL SKIN TYPES TO REDUCE PUFFINESS AND DARK CIRCLES AROUND THE EYE AREA

Booster
+ **10% Azelaic Acid Booster**
+ **C15 Super Booster**
+ **C25 Super Booster**

Treatment
+ **CLINICAL Triple Action Dark Spot Eraser 7% AHA and 2% Hydroquinone Lotion**
  (only for stubborn brown discoloration under the eye area, not for puffiness)
+ **CLINICAL 20% Niacinamide Treatment**

Eye Cream or Eye Gel
+ **CLINICAL Ceramide-Enriched Eye Cream**
+ **RESIST Anti-Aging Eye Gel** (great for reducing puffiness)
+ **RESIST Anti-Aging Eye Cream**
+ **Omega + Complex Eye Cream**

Sunscreen
+ **DEFENSE Essential Glow Moisturizer SPF 30**
+ **SKIN RECOVERY Daily Moisturizing Lotion SPF 30**
+ **HYDRALIGHT Shine-Free Mineral Complex SPF 30**
+ **CALM Mineral Moisturizer SPF 30 Normal to Dry Skin**

CHAPTER 16

SUPERHERO INGREDIENTS

SOME INGREDIENTS ARE WORTH EXTRA ATTENTION

We've talked a lot in this book about categories of skin care ingredients, such as antioxidants, skin-replenishing ingredients, and skin-restoring ingredients, along with AHAs, BHA, and, lest we forget, sunscreen. We've repeatedly said there is no best ingredient for skin; rather, there are dozens and dozens of them, and they are synergistically better when used together. That is still 100% true.

What we're about to go over may seem contradictory, but there are indeed some superhero ingredients in skin care that deserve individual attention because of their outstanding properties. It doesn't mean that everyone has to use every one of them or that those that address your concerns must be used every day. However, depending on your skin concerns, some should be among the products you use, and sometimes they should be present at high concentrations.

Although AHAs, BHA, and sunscreen actives are some of the most unique, valuable, superhero ingredients in skin care, and we've discussed them well enough throughout this book that you won't find them yet again on this list. (See? We do know when to let up!)

VITAMIN C

Vitamin C is present naturally in younger skin. It is one of skin's major sources of antioxidant protection, but, because of sun damage and age, your skin gets to the point where it can't produce enough vitamin C to keep it healthy and protected from the environment.

Skin needs to be well supplied with vitamin C, but when skin can't make enough on its own, topically applied vitamin C can deliver the same benefits.

Vitamin C often is listed on ingredient labels as ascorbic acid, among various other names (though ascorbic acid is considered the most bio-available form), and the products with high concentrations (up to 25%) have impressive efficacy without tipping the scale toward irritation. Aside from environmental protection, research has also shown that vitamin C can improve an uneven skin tone and brighten dull skin, making it visibly more radiant, just like younger skin.

RESVERATROL

Resveratrol is a superhero due to its extremely potent polyphenolic antioxidant properties. Resveratrol is found naturally in red grapes, red wine, nuts, and fruits such as blueberries and cranberries.

Applied topically, resveratrol helps protect skin's surface, interrupts and helps rebuff negative environmental influences, and brightens a tired-looking complexion. It also has significant skin-calming properties that may help minimize redness.

Although applying plant extracts that contain resveratrol can be helpful, the pure form is more bio-available and more stable, which means it works far better than just the plant extract alone.

GREEN TEA AND EGCG

Green tea is an exceptionally effective antioxidant when applied topically. A significant amount of research has established green tea's ability to restore skin and protect it from environmental damage, and it also can provide distinct skin-calming properties. Much like any antioxidant, the properties found in plants are great, but the actual antioxidant component itself is the most potent and stable for skin. The main compound in green tea that provides its antioxidant kick is epigallocatechin gallate (EGCG). When this ingredient is present in skin care products, it's more potent and more bio-available than whole green tea extract would be to diminish free radical damage and reduce inflammation. It can even help control oily skin!

NIACINAMIDE (VITAMIN B3)

There are lots of ingredients we can wax poetic about and niacinamide is one of them; in some ways it stands out as one of the best. Over the years, research has established niacinamide as an important ingredient for minimizing enlarged pores, reducing clogged pores and blackheads, and strengthening skin's all-important barrier, and, in high concentrations, resolving oil-related bumps. Current research shows that it is even more impressive than the original research indicated. Niacinamide has extraordinary anti-aging benefits. Along with reducing pore size and tightening sagging pores (which we love), it meaningfully diminishes the appearance of wrinkles, restores an even skin tone, and increases hydration because it stimulates the natural production of ceramide and keratin in skin. Higher concentrations (10-20%) of niacinamide are necessary for stubborn skin concerns, especially clogged pores.

BLENDS OF CONCENTRATED NON-FRAGRANT PLANT OILS

Various non-fragrant oils can have immediate and long-lasting replenishing, nourishing, anti-redness, and antioxidant advantages for skin. We can't stress this enough: These oils must be non-fragrant because aromatic essential oils have inflammatory properties that are a problem for skin.

The non-fragrant superhero plant oils are a perfect way to soothe skin, provide immediate relief for rough, tight, dry skin on the face or around the eye area, and ease redness and sensitivity. They can be used in their pure form all over your skin or as a spot solution over dehydrated areas. Plant oils are also included in serums, moisturizers, and sunscreens.

Some of the most notable non-fragrant plant oils for skin include jojoba seed oil, safflower seed oil, apricot kernel oil, sunflower seed oil, cranberry seed oil, argan kernel oil, borage seed oil, evening primrose oil, rosehip oil (not to be confused with fragrant rose oil), marula oil, tamanu oil, hemp seed oil, pomegranate seed oil, flaxseed oil, and chia seed oil.

And, despite what you may have read, there is no best one. The claims about certain oils having miraculous properties are overblown and untrue; they're not any more useful than other oils. In other words, there is no remarkable advantage to argan oil versus ordinary sounding safflower oil. Their beneficial components are not significantly different, and each has value on its own or when blended with others in a formula. That's why we love oil blends: You get the benefits of all the non-fragrant oils plus the nuances that make each oil distinct (not better, just different). Think of it like salad greens that are exceptionally nutritious on their own, but that your body is even happier with when you add vegetables of other colors into the mix!

HYALURONIC ACID

Hyaluronic acid, a naturally occurring substance, is the key molecule involved in skin hydration. It is known for its unique capacity to attract and hold a balanced amount of water in all layers of skin, not just on the surface. But, as is true for most things that affect skin, sun damage and age prevent skin from making enough hyaluronic acid to keep it properly hydrated (and hydrated skin is always a sign of good skin health).

The statistic often stated about hyaluronic acid is that it can hold onto 1,000x its molecular weight in water. For example, it's been said that 0.03 ounces of hyaluronic acid can hold up to 1.5 gallons of water. Some researchers say that that amount is overstated, but even if hyaluronic acid can hold only half that much water, that's still a whole lot of water. It's hard to grasp how that works for skin because we know that too much water in skin can break down skin's barrier and weaken its protective and resilient properties.

The reason hyaluronic acid doesn't end up drowning skin by holding too much water is because it's a "smart" ingredient. Skin is made up of multiple layers and the interplay between them is complex, but because hyaluronic acid has cell-communicating properties, it knows how to distribute hydration evenly throughout skin. This form of hydration improves resiliency, reduces dryness, and provides a radiant glow. Hyaluronic acid is the best kind of superhero, as is its salt form, known as sodium hyaluronate.

CERAMIDES

Ceramides are the most abundant part of skin's structure, making up over 50% of its composition. They're critical for holding skin together and protecting it from dehydration, signs of sensitivity, and environmental attack.

What makes ceramides even more amazing is not only the role they play in protecting skin, but also the role they play in "educating" skin, literally helping it look younger and feel better. Ceramides, along with retinol, niacinamide, hyaluronic acid, and peptides, are all responsible for intelligent skin communication. Each works in a specific way to normalize or repair impaired physiological processes in skin. Ceramides applied to skin have their own way of doing that.

When we're young, skin makes lots and lots of ceramides, but because of, you guessed it, sun damage and age, both the quantity and quality of the ceramides in our skin decreases. Providing skin with the ceramides it no longer can produce for itself significantly improves skin's structure, enhances its ability to defend itself from environmental damage, and prevents moisture loss. The best way to deliver ceramides to skin is via skin care products that contain these precious ingredients, although research has shown that oral intake of ceramides (in supplement form) is also beneficial.

There are several types of ceramides; research is still ongoing to determine exactly how many different types are present in skin and which ones are the best. For now, we know there are eight important ceramides, two of the better-known are ceramide EOP and ceramide NP (the initials indicate their chemical composition), but all ceramides are clearly valuable for skin.

There are also two fascinating adjunct ingredients to ceramides that are sometimes included in skin care products: phytosphingosine and sphingolipids. Both help skin make more of the specific ceramides it needs. These types of formulary combinations present exciting possibilities to address signs of aging and to help protect skin from environmental stressors.

CANNABIDIOL (CBD) FOR SKIN CARE

The emerging science and the explosion in the number of products claiming to contain cannabidiol (CBD) means that there are no easy answers when it comes to how it benefits your skin. CBD is a component of the marijuana and hemp plants, both members of the plant genus *Cannabis*. The difficulty involved in sorting this all out is due to the enormous amount of conflicting information in the research and the endless websites and brands claiming to have the answers.

The bottom line: Yes, CBD isolate (meaning pure CBD) and full-spectrum CBD (meaning the source contains cannabidiol and other beneficial compounds, but mostly CBD) are great for skin because of their amazing calming properties.

Without question, reducing inflammation is one of the most important needs for skin because everything, from wrinkles, brown spots, sagging, acne, rosacea, to microbiome damage—all are due to inflammation. Anything you can do to reduce inflammation is brilliant for skin. However, when it comes to CBD, you'll get this benefit only if the product really contains CBD. Therein lies the problem, because not all products claiming to contain CBD actually do!

For products claiming to contain CBD, the FDA-regulated name that should be on the ingredient label is *cannabidiol* (this regulated labeling is called the International Nomenclature of Cosmetic Ingredients [INCI]). Any other name on an ingredient label, such as "CBD-enriched hemp seed oil," does not necessarily indicate that the product actually contains cannabidiol. Regardless, to be 100% certain, you can always ask the company for their product's specification, which is called an "assay." If they won't share the assay with you, or say they don't have it, move on.

CBD works as a cell-communicating ingredient. It literally "tells" the natural cannabinoid receptors in skin to reduce inflammation in a unique way; that is, it works in a manner different from other calming ingredients. That's a good thing, because the more ways you can reduce inflammation in skin, the better, which is why you should *never* rely only on CBD or on any other single ingredient to reduce exposome inflammation.

Here's how it works: All cells, including skin cells, have receptor sites. These sites respond to millions of specific substances, telling the cell what to do. In the case of skin cells, those substances include vitamin A (retinol or other retinoids), dozens of different peptides, ceramides, niacinamide, licorice extract, adenosine, lecithin, willowherb, and various others, including CBD.

Skin cells have two receptor sites for CBD, known as CB1 and CB2. When CBD absorbs into skin, it locates these sites on the skin cell and tells the cell to diminish the damage caused by inflammation. Given that signs of aging, sun damage, acne, skin discolorations, rosacea, sensitivity, and on and on are all stimulated and made worse by inflammation, an ingredient (in this case CBD) capable of directly "telling" skin to reduce inflammation is a great benefit, improving almost every aspect of skin's health and appearance.

PEPTIDES

Peptides are a fascinating group of ingredients, backed by research that proves they have impressive benefits for addressing a variety of skin concerns. Whether you're struggling with wrinkles, loss of firmness, discolorations, dehydration, dullness, and on and on, there are peptides that can make a visible difference. Although peptides are found naturally in skin, the ones contained in skin care products are bio-engineered to target specific aspects of skin function, remain stable in a formulation, and are made without animal-derived ingredients. Despite information you may have seen to the contrary, peptides can be used with any other skin care ingredient, including AHAs and BHA. The skin is acidic, so the acidity of the AHAs or BHA does not affect the efficacy of the peptides.

Each peptide (there are dozens of them, and more are being created in labs) is designed to deliver its benefit precisely where it will do the most good. For that to happen, each peptide must be able to penetrate skin's uppermost layers so it can begin "teaching" skin how to fix aspects of itself that are acting older and not behaving in a healthy manner. Depending on the type of peptide or the combination of peptides in a product, they can target loss of firmness, dullness, uneven skin tone, skin strength, or hydration pathways, and they can trigger the creation of other vital substances in skin. Sometimes they send a direct message, sometimes they send a special signal that other cells pick up on and respond to favorably.

OMEGA FATTY ACIDS

Omega fatty acids are found in many foods, including fish oil and plant oils. They're known for their considerable nutritional benefits when consumed as part of a healthy diet. What you might not know is that they also have intriguing benefits when applied to skin!

There are 11 omega fatty acids; the most vital for skin are omega-3, omega-6, and omega-9. Omega fatty acids, among skin's foremost protectors from environmental damage, are capable of calming external and internal stressors that cause redness and sensitivity. When all three omega fatty acids are present in your diet or if you topically apply products that are rich in omega fatty acids, they enhance and resupply skin's surface layers, keep skin hydrated, and improve healthy skin function. Sources of omega fatty acids for topical use include chia, flax (linseed), and hemp seed oils, passionflower oil, alpha linolenic acid, olive oil, borage oil, among others.

Omega fatty acids have a natural affinity for skin, and are exponentially beneficial when combined with other skin-loving ingredients like ceramides, cholesterol, and glycerin.

RETINOL

Retinol, one of the superhero ingredients for skin, has been around for a long time, and, in many ways, stands out from the rest. Products that contain retinol, whether a high concentration or low concentration, aren't a miracle for skin, but they come pretty darn close (even formulas with low concentrations have demonstrated impressive efficacy). The best concentration for you to use depends on your skin concerns. If you have advanced signs of aging, skin discolorations, uneven skin tone, or clogged pores, high concentrations (0.5-1%) are better; if prevention is the goal, low concentrations (0.01-0.1%) are perfect.

Retinol is the technical name for the entire vitamin A molecule. When applied topically, it is the preeminent skin-restoring ingredient. Retinol sends repair signals throughout the layers of skin, and skin essentially "listens" and responds to that message by going to work to start repairing damage, especially sun damage, and teaching skin to behave in a more healthy manner.

As wonderful as retinol is for skin, you must remain realistic—skin can recover only so much from past damage and the effects of aging. However, there is no question that skin does much better with retinol helping than it does without it.

Retinol, over the years, has gained much-deserved fame for what it can do for skin, but along with that fame has come lots of misleading information and myths. One of the major myths we'd like to bust right now is the fear that retinol may be too strong for your skin and cause problems—that is an exaggerated piece of skin care nonsense. Skin can be sensitive to just about anything you put on it, from plant extracts to sunscreen ingredients, vitamin C, and on and on. Retinol is no exception; some people may find their skin doesn't like retinol. Therefore, just as with any skin care ingredient or skin care product, even the best of the best, not everyone can use everything.

The other myth about retinol is that it helps skin exfoliate so you don't need an AHA or BHA exfoliant—that isn't true. AHAs and BHA work very differently from retinol, and complement each other when paired in a complete skin care routine—they do not replace each other.

The confusion arises because, for some people, retinol can cause irritation, which in turn may cause skin to flake. However, this flaking side effect (which should be temporary because skin usually acclimates to the retinol's activity in improving cell function) is not the same as exfoliation. Regardless of the product, *don't mistake flaking for exfoliation*. When healthy, normal exfoliation is taking place, you shouldn't be able to see it (as in skin flaking off) or feel it.

There are several reasons why you might experience flaking or irritation after using a retinol product (or any superhero ingredient for that matter). For example, you might be using a retinol product that is poorly formulated or one that contains irritating ingredients. Or you might have selected retinol products that contain too much retinol for your skin, causing a sensitized reaction.

Another thing to consider: You might be using retinol along with other products that contain too high a concentration of other bio-active ingredients. Although such a combination works for many people, it might be too intense for you. Often, a reaction occurs because you're using a retinol product along with other skin care products that contain irritating or harsh ingredients.

Another reason retinol might not be for you is that you are one of the small percentage of people whose skin can't tolerate retinol, in any amount or any format. If that's you, don't be discouraged, as there many other exciting anti-aging ingredients to try! Retinol is great, but it isn't the only one.

AZELAIC ACID

It's a mystery why some great skin care ingredients fly under the radar, despite long-standing research proving they are more than worthy of your attention. Azelaic acid is one of those ingredients! Decades of research have shown that azelaic acid can reduce the appearance of blemishes, help fade post-acne marks, brighten an uneven skin tone, interrupt environmental damage (especially skin discolorations), refine skin's surface because it has some exfoliating properties, and considerably improve redness, regardless of why your face is red. Wow!

Azelaic acid can be derived from grains like barley, wheat, and rye, but a lab-engineered form is used in skin care products because of its stability and effectiveness. Much of the research on azelaic acid has involved prescription-only topical concentrations of 15% to 20%, but azelaic acid also has incredible benefits at lower concentrations.

If you're wondering whether to seek an over-the-counter cosmetic azelaic acid skin care product or a prescription version, research shows that a 10% concentration, which is available in over-the-counter products, can improve skin concerns similarly to higher concentrations! Another way to choose is to assess your skin care concerns. If you have advanced signs of aging, skin discolorations, uneven skin tone, or clogged pores, higher concentrations are better. If prevention is the goal, lower concentrations are perfect.

BEAUTY SUPPLEMENTS INGREDIENTS

Whether or not you should take "beauty" supplements to help your skin has been a contentious issue for years, and we consistently challenge such claims when the research is lacking. Over the past few years, compelling research has provided insight into the issue of beauty supplements. Although that doesn't mean there still aren't lingering questions, the positives clearly outweigh the doubts.

Some of the debate is centered on the fact that supplements of any kind tend to be overused or aren't necessary, or that the research is biased or incomplete. Then there are the ludicrous claims that many companies make about their supplements. And there are lots of nutrition experts and scientists who would say that a healthy diet is far better than a supplement any day. On the other hand, there are many who would assert that a healthy diet can never be diverse enough or complete enough to address the extensive needs of the body and skin as it ages.

From the research we've pored over, both positions turn out to be 100% right. If you don't eat a healthy diet and live a healthy lifestyle, you can't expect any supplement to make up for not taking good care of your body. You can't eat sugars, saturated fats, and foods that lack nutritional value, or smoke cigarettes or marijuana (yes, smoking marijuana puts carcinogens into your throat and lungs, just like smoking cigarettes), and then expect supplements to undo or prevent the damage.

On the other hand, because the quantity of food we would need to eat to get the ideal amounts of all the substances current research shows are best for building collagen, maintaining hydration, and significantly helping your body and skin combat environmental damage is too much for most people, supplements can be undeniably helpful. Combined with a healthy diet and a healthy lifestyle, supplements can be a brilliant way to make sure you're getting enough of what your body and skin need to stay young and vital.

The question is: What are the most significant supplements associated with helping skin? Given that we know the benefits of supplements for your heart, eyes, or better digestion, the same is now true for skin. We now know what supplements can maintain and create a stronger, more protective barrier, what supplements can reinforce youthful support structures like collagen and elastin, and which antioxidants can interrupt environmental damage.

The most significant supplements for skin are a range of stable, potent antioxidants, ceramides, hyaluronic acid, peptides, collagen, and omega fatty acids, all of which are well-established as providing benefit. As more research comes to light, you can expect this list to grow.

When it comes to antioxidants in a supplement, one of the best ways to judge their efficacy is the ORAC (oxygen radical absorbance capacity) rating. The ORAC rating of various foods or supplements scores how effective they are in reducing inflammation and free radical damage, which are the primary reasons why skin ages. Not surprisingly, many nutrient-dense foods, like dark-colored fruits and vegetables, have very high ORAC scores.

Taking daily oral supplements of these superhero ingredients benefits the body, and also has been shown to benefit skin, increasing skin's firmness, hydration, smoothness, providing protection from the environment, and even protecting skin from sun damage (but don't take that to mean you can forgo sunscreen!).

CHAPTER 17

PREBIOTICS, PROBIOTICS, AND POSTBIOTICS

IT BEGINS WITH YOUR SKIN'S MICROBIOME

Probiotics are essential for your body's overall health, but using probiotics to maintain healthy, younger skin is a relatively new concept. It's one of the more complicated subjects in skin care, but hang in there, we'll get you through it.

Before we share what probiotics and other "biotics" are and how they work on skin and in the body, it's essential to first discuss what's known as the microbiome.

Human microbiomes (a microbiome is the unique collection of organisms in a given environment such as the digestive system or skin) are fascinating areas of study, each with massive amounts of research and new assessments coming to light on a regular basis. When it comes to skin and probiotics, there is still a lot we don't know, but there is also a lot we *do* know. And the research is not only about probiotics, it's also about prebiotics and postbiotics. Understanding how the pieces of the microbiome puzzle fit together will help you take good care of it and avoid wasting your money on products that can't help.

THE MICROBIOME'S PRE-, PRO-, AND POSTBIOTICS

Your skin's microbiome is made up of "good" and "bad" microbes that live on its surface. **Probiotics** are the living microbes (bacteria and yeast) that exist on skin. **Prebiotics** are the substances on skin that help feed and encourage the growth and healthy balance of probiotics. **Postbiotics** are the byproducts (new substances) that probiotics generate. Probiotics get most of the attention, but as it turns out, prebiotics and postbiotics play an even more vital role in skin care.

The topic of pre-, pro-, and postbiotics for skin care could be summed up by asking how "dirty" does your skin need to be? After all, when you think of bacteria and yeast living on your skin, that certainly doesn't sound clean! Most people would reach for a disinfectant. But to help support the fight against signs of aging, acne, inflammation, some skin disorders, environmental damage, or dehydration, and to strengthen and maintain skin's barrier requires skin to be pretty darn "dirty." Ironically, a disinfectant would destabilize your microbiome. The goal is to have a balanced and thriving microbiome.

How to go about being appropriately "dirty" is where skin care can help. But first, you need to understand what is meant by "dirty," as that will help you understand the role that pre-, pro-, and postbiotics play for your skin.

WHY A BALANCED MICROBIOME IS IMPORTANT FOR SKIN

Skin begins creating its microbiome at birth, continues to grow and change as we age, and then stabilizes in adulthood. What makes the skin's microbiome unstable is almost always some type of inflammation, whether internal (skin disorders, pH imbalance, disease) or external (pollution, sun damage, irritating skin care products).

When the microbiome is stable and balanced, all the microbes living on the skin and in the pores and sweat glands digest (literally eat) some of the skin's content of oils, fatty acids, proteins, and dead skin cells. After the microbes are done eating, they produce vital byproducts called postbiotics. Skin needs these postbiotics to be healthy.

What does it mean when you have a healthy, balanced microbiome? Some of the microbes on skin are helpful, while some are (or can become) harmful. The good microbes are often referred to as "resident bacteria," while the bad microbes are called "transient bacteria."

Oddly enough, when skin's microbiome is out of balance, the good microbes can become bad and the bad ones can become good (yes, we know, this makes us scratch our heads, too, but facts are facts). This means that a balanced microbiome must have the good *and* the bad to keep everything in harmony. It's not about getting rid of all the bad bacteria so the good can flourish; doing so would have a negative effect!

When skin's microbiome is balanced, the good and bad microorganisms keep each other in check, working together to create postbiotics, which include peptides, proteins, amino acids, enzymes, hyaluronic acid, lactic acid, ceramides, antioxidants, and other substances that are vitally important for skin. We find that simply amazing! The postbiotic substances that the probiotics generate do the following:

+ Strengthen the skin's surface to protect against environmental damage.
+ Enhance skin's ability to become—and stay—properly hydrated.
+ Diminish factors that trigger sensitized, reddened skin.
+ Restore and maintain a healthy pH balance on skin's surface.

WHAT CAUSES YOUR SKIN'S MICROBIOME TO BECOME UNBALANCED?

Many things affect your skin's microbiome, so many that it's a bit overwhelming. What we know for certain is that anything that causes skin inflammation throws the microbiome into a state of confusion, which can become a vicious cycle, and it's not easy to get it back in balance. Sun damage, irritating skin care products, an unhealthy diet, smoking, hormonal skin disorders, immune-related skin disorders, wounds, and illness all can obstruct the microbiome's efforts to remain balanced.

We actually were surprised when we uncovered the research indicating that ingredients such as retinoids, niacinamide, sunscreen ingredients, and benzoyl peroxide, among others, did not disturb the skin's microbiome. Most likely that's because all of these ingredients have calming and anything that reduces or prevents skin reactiveness helps stabilize the microbiome.

CAN APPLYING PROBIOTICS TO SKIN BALANCE ITS MICROBIOME?

You can absolutely help balance your skin's microbiome, but not with probiotics alone. Rather, it takes a combination of pre-, pro-, and postbiotics to get results. Just applying probiotics can't balance your microbiome because of sheer numbers: first, there are billions of us in the world and every person has a different, ever-changing microbiome composed of billions of probiotics on our skin. No product can know exactly what one's skin needs.

When it comes to skin, even if everyone had the exact same microbiome, how would any skin care product know which of the trillions of microbes on your skin were out of balance? And given that "bad" biotics are as important as "good" biotics, it would be unconscionable to formulate a skin care product that contained bad strains, such as *Staphylococcus* or *Streptococcus* bacteria. Yet, even those infectious bacteria are a natural part of everyone's microbiome!

Another serious limitation for probiotic skin care products, in terms of balancing skin's microbiome, is the fact that the microbiome needs living, thriving bacteria, viruses, yeast, fungus, and other microorganisms (the good and the bad) to function as it should. Water-based skin care products are formulated with preservatives to prevent any kind of microorganism from growing out of control, so a responsible formula would kill the living probiotics it contained.

Claims related to balancing skin's microbiome are really about what *prebiotics* can do to balance skin's microbiome and what *postbiotics* can deliver to skin.

SO, WHAT *CAN* APPLYING PROBIOTICS DO FOR SKIN?

Although probiotics themselves cannot balance skin's microbiome, they do have benefit. Research has shown that numerous probiotics and probiotic-derived ingredients have distinct benefits when it comes to reducing inflammation and improving signs of skin concerns, particularly acne and eczema (a type of atopic dermatitis).

There is a problem, however, in that not all the research agrees with this, and most of the research didn't look at the same probiotic or probiotic derivatives. Another issue is that the studies were done on animals or in a laboratory, not on people; were not done with a placebo control (that is, one product with the probiotic was applied on one person and another product without the probiotic was applied on the other person); or were not done blind (that is, the researcher was not informed about who was getting which treatment). These are major limitations when trying to draw conclusions about which probiotics can be beneficial.

Having said that, there *is* agreement about a handful of probiotics and probiotic derivatives (often referred to as "lysates") that can have benefit for skin when applied topically because of their stability and their ability to reduce inflammation on skin. Proven probiotics include the species *Lactobacillus acidophilus* and *Bifidobacteria bifidum*. It's interesting to note that the "lysate" form means the probiotics are dead, but they retain many of the skin-friendly benefits of living probiotics.

WHAT ARE PREBIOTICS FOR SKIN?

As mentioned above, skin care products that contain prebiotics are a good way to establish a healthy microbiome because applying such products helps your skin make exactly the probiotics it needs. That way your skin is better able to reinforce its microbiome's natural balance.

Prebiotics for skin are carbohydrate-based, often in the form of sugars. Plant extracts with prebiotics that can be included in skin care products include oats, barley, wheat bran, asparagus, onion, banana, and a plant fiber known as inulin, which is found in chicory root. Even better for skin when applied topically are prebiotic plant sugars, such as xylitol, rhamnose, and a large group of ingredients known as fructooligosaccharides, which are potent sources of prebiotics (they're also natural hydrators) and, therefore, have an inherent capacity to help generate probiotics. To sum it up: Prebiotics work beautifully as an energy source to help skin make the specific probiotics it needs.

WHAT ABOUT POSTBIOTICS?

When the microbiome is balanced (at least for as long as it can remain balanced, which isn't easy due to environmental assault), the probiotics living on skin produce the valuable substances we mentioned above. Together, with the postbiotics, they help keep skin hydrated, strengthened, and protected from the environment. They also help reduce redness, diminish acne, and improve other skin concerns.

However, because you can't really tell if your microbiome is balanced or not and because of pollution, sun damage, and skin disorders, you can safely assume that your microbiome is generally out of balance. An imbalanced microbiome can't create those great ingredients for skin. Giving your skin the substances a healthy microbiome would make on its own by applying skin care products that contain them is the perfect solution to this problem.

Of course, it's helpful to do what you can to keep your microbiome as balanced as possible. The best way to do that is to use a product that contains a mix of prebiotics, probiotics, and postbiotics in a cream, lotion, or serum (it's up to you which texture you prefer) as part of a complete skin care routine, which, of course, includes daily sun protection.

CHAPTER 18

POLLUTION, BLUE LIGHT, AND DETOXING

AIR POLLUTION IS A PROBLEM FOR SKIN

No matter where we live, air pollution, to some degree, poses serious risks to our health. New and ongoing research explains how airborne pollutants affect how your skin looks and feels, and even how it ages.

Some research suggests that pollution is just as bad for skin as unprotected sun exposure. The need to protect skin from environmental pollution—not just from UV light—is more important now than ever before as our planet becomes more polluted. The right skin care is where that protection begins.

WHAT IS AIR POLLUTION?

Air pollution refers to the gases or particles released into the air by human activity, such as exhaust from automobiles, pollutants from manufacturing processes and chemical and petroleum refineries, cigarette smoke, and many others. Most gaseous airborne pollutants don't penetrate skin immediately; instead, they trigger a cascade of damage on skin's surface, and eventually, that damage makes it easier for the pollutants to get into your body.

One type of nongaseous pollutant, known as small particulate matter, is small enough to get into pores, where it becomes trapped and causes ongoing damage. (These pollutants are often referred to as nanoparticles because they're so tiny.) Simply washing your face doesn't remove these pollution particles once they get into the pores, although facial cleansing does remove larger surface pollutants.

Although air pollution is worse in and around big cities, living in rural areas doesn't mean you're free from risk. All forms of pollution move through the atmosphere and bodies of water, and can settle in soil, so it easily travels beyond the borders of industrialized areas. There also are multiple factors that contribute to pollution within your household, including the cleaning products you use, how you cook your food, and things like aerosol sprays (think hairspray).

HOW ENVIRONMENTAL POLLUTION AFFECTS SKIN

Scientific research has revealed how ongoing, daily exposure to pollution negatively affects skin's health and appearance. The five major types of air pollution that pose the biggest risk to your skin's appearance include:

1. Automobile and truck exhaust
2. Cigarette smoke or vaping
3. Manufacturing byproducts (such as phthalates from plastics)
4. Small particulate matter (including many volatile organic compounds in the form of aerosols)
5. Smog and the dangerous ground-level ozone it generates

All forms of pollution cause free radical damage to skin. Left unchecked, this damage leads to the breakdown and deterioration of everything skin needs to look healthy and prevent signs of aging.

Pollution also throws skin's microbiome out of balance by disrupting its barrier, which exacerbates the effects of all types of air pollution. The list of problems that airborne pollutants cause is staggering:

+ Brown spots
+ Uneven, dull skin tone
+ Breakdown of skin's supportive structures
+ Enlarged pores
+ Clogged pores
+ Sensitive, redness-prone skin
+ Uncomfortable dry, itchy skin

The small airborne pollutants that get stuck in pores can cause acne-like breakouts for those prone to acne (often called chemical- or pollution-induced acne) and can trigger damage in the deeper layers of skin, right where wrinkles and most discolorations form.

As mentioned above, when skin's surface breaks down, many types of airborne pollutants are small enough to get into the body through the impaired skin. That's another reason why it's so important to keep skin's surface intact and healthy.

Despite what you may have heard or read, toxins from pollution don't get past the surface layers of skin or beyond the interior of the pore, but they do a lot of indirect damage in those areas. Breathing and eating are direct routes for pollutants to enter your body; you can help reduce the damage by not smoking and by eating a diet rich in antioxidants. The same is true for skin: There are very important skin care steps you can take to limit environmental damage to your skin.

HOW TO PROTECT SKIN FROM POLLUTION

Although pollution is too pervasive for you to completely protect skin from all its visible effects, the right skin care products can make a significant difference. What *can* you do to shield your skin, as much as possible, from airborne pollutants and the effects they trigger? The answer: Use skin care products filled to the brim with proven anti-pollution ingredients, such as antioxidants, like those from dark-colored fruits and vegetables, that interrupt or neutralize the cascade of damage.

Products formulated with antioxidants that interrupt the process of pollution's effects on skin are critical to reducing the damage, but as you already know, it takes more than antioxidants. Your pollution-fighting products should also include potent, soothing ingredients that neutralize the inflammation caused by air pollutants, and skin-replenishing ingredients like ceramides to fortify and strengthen skin's surface so it can do its own job of protecting itself (weakened, damaged skin is more vulnerable to all environmental assaults).

It's also important to use a leave-on AHA or BHA exfoliant because they help dislodge the pollutants that get trapped inside pores. Skin-brightening ingredients also are helpful because pollution has clearly been shown to discolor and darken skin, no matter your ethnicity or age.

RECOMMENDED PRODUCTS FROM PAULA'S CHOICE SKINCARE TO HELP PROTECT SKIN FROM POLLUTION AND ENVIRONMENTAL DAMAGE

Cleanser
+ **DEFENSE Hydrating Gel-to-Cream Cleanser**

Serum
+ **DEFENSE Antioxidant Pore Purifier**
+ **DEFENSE Triple Algae Pollution Shield**
+ **Omega+ Complex Serum**
+ **EARTH SOURCED Power Berry Serum**

Daytime Moisturizers with SPF
+ **DEFENSE Essential Glow Moisturizer SPF 30**

Nighttime Moisturizer
+ **DEFENSE Nightly Reconditioning Moisturizer**
+ **Omega + Complex Moisturizer**

DOES BLUE LIGHT HURT YOUR SKIN?

Yes, blue light does hurt your skin, and that's the type of light emitted by your digital devices, and it can cause damage! The science of light is amazing. There is visible light (like blue light) and there is invisible light you *can't* see, like the UVA and UVB rays from the sun that cause sunburn and other forms of serious damage. There also are light rays you *do* see that come from the sun, but that also are emitted by most digital devices, including your smartphone.

If you look at a chart about the sun's damaging UVA and UVB rays, you'll see that their wavelengths range from 280 nm to 400 nm ("nm" stands for nanometer, which is a measurement of length). Next on the spectrum is blue light, whose wavelength ranges from 380 nm to 500 nm. (The entire light spectrum goes up to 700 nm.) As mentioned, the blue light portion is what emanates from digital devices, such as computers, flat-screen LED TVs, fluorescent light bulbs, and smartphones.

Evolving research has shown that blue light can be bad for skin. It's certain that blue light in the 380–400 nm range is problematic, although the risk seems to lessen somewhat toward the top end at 500 nm. Long-term exposure to concentrated blue light energy can cause skin damage, including color changes, inflammation, and weakening of skin's surface. Blue light promotes stressors in skin that cause photo-aging; that is, aging from exposure to light.

Without question, sunlight is the primary source of the blue light to which we are exposed; digital devices emit only a fraction of the amount of the sun's blue light radiation. However, although the sun's blue light is a concern, our phones are much closer to us than the sun, and this "close-up" exposure matters.

We spend a lot of time using our devices, holding them close to our face and eyes, and it adds up—that's where health issues arise. Statistics show that millennials check their smartphones 157 times per day, in comparison to older adults, who check their phones only about 30 times per day. That means millennials are at a much higher risk of blue light exposure *each and every day*.

When it comes to your eyes, there's a good bit of research showing how damaging unprotected exposure to blue light can be. The research into blue light damaging skin, however, is far less conclusive, but still a concern. That's because, while there is research that definitely shows blue light hurts skin, there's also research showing it can be helpful. For example, certain blue light treatments can be a potentially effective therapy for some skin disorders. Confusing, yes, but emerging research is often that way, and this is a new area of study.

Most smartphones, laptops, and tablets have a setting that disables blue light in favor of yellow light (often called night mode or nightshift), which is not damaging to your eyes or your skin. If your devices, especially your mobile phone, have this feature, using it all the time is a mandatory skin- and vision-saving step.

If your phone, tablet, laptop, or desk monitors don't have a yellow light setting, you can cover your screens with a blue light screen shield (Amazon.com has plenty of options). It's a cheap fix and it eliminates the worry about skin care or sunglasses when using your phone or tablet (if only it were that easy for your skin and the sun).

Regarding the positive effect that blue light can have on skin, there are other ways to care for skin that don't have the negative effects of blue light! Trying to solve one problem while causing another is not good skin care.

CAN YOU DETOX SKIN?

No, you can't. Detoxifying facial masks and other treatments that promise to purge skin of toxins may sound impressive, but the reality is far from it. Products labeled with claims such as "detox for acne" are even more misleading, and infuriating, because they often leave breakout-prone skin in *worse shape*. Let's set the record straight on skin detoxes once and for all.

THE TRUTH ABOUT TOXINS

Toxins are produced by just about everything: plants, animals, insects, industrial waste, people, smoking, garbage, automobiles, and on and on and on. Despite what you may have heard, toxins do not, and cannot, leave your body through the pores—it's **physiologically impossible**. The job of eliminating toxins falls primarily to your kidneys and liver, the body's detoxifying organs. Both do a pretty good job on their own, as long as you're healthy.

There are a few studies indicating that sweat (*not* skin or pores) can serve as a carrier in "detoxifying" by removing toxins, for example, trace heavy metals, from the body. However, before you jump into the sauna to "sweat those toxins out of your body," you should be aware that third-party experts consider the methodology of those studies to be questionable at best.

Even if it were possible to eliminate toxins through sweat, many are usually present only in trace amounts, which means they are pretty much meaningless for the health of your body. And besides, you will quickly be resupplied with toxins as soon as you breathe.

THE TRUTH ABOUT DETOXIFYING SKIN CARE

We've already established that toxins cannot be purged via your pores or skin, but, making the issue of "detoxing skin" even more absurd is that no one ever specifies which toxins are being eliminated or identifies the research on which their claims are based. That's because there is no research showing you can purge toxins from your skin. It's always best to stick with the physiological facts about skin and what the research says really works. So, ignore the detoxing skin claims because they aren't going to help your skin or your wallet.

That said, there is a huge difference between products that claim to *purge* skin of toxins and products that can help *defend* skin from what the toxins in the environment do to skin. Antioxidants and many other beneficial ingredients really can help defend against the negative effects of environmental toxins by interrupting the free radical damage and skin changes they cause. The key is to make sure you use such products as part of your daily routine.

During the day use a sunscreen enriched with antioxidants, so you're getting double the benefit (sun protection + environmental protection); at night use products loaded with antioxidants that will defend your skin while you sleep. *BUT*, despite claims to the contrary, the truth in beauty is that there is no way to purge toxins through your skin, it just is not physiologically possible.

ABOUT THE AUTHORS

Paula Begoun, Bryan Barron, and Desiree Stordahl are internationally recognized for their objective, candid, and extensive research-backed knowledge on skin care and cosmetic ingredients. Together they have sold millions of books worldwide on the subject of beauty. Over the years, their work as consumer advocates has been featured on TV shows such as Oprah, CNN, The Today Show, The Dr. Oz Show, 20/20, Dateline NBC, and The View as well as hundreds of other appearances and media interviews around the globe. It's their honor and privilege to help people understand how to get their best skin.